题源之间

26天拓宽英语阅读边界

主编 边明锐 薛非

北京理工大学出版社
BEIJING INSTITUTE OF TECHNOLOGY PRESS

版权专有 侵权必究

图书在版编目（CIP）数据

题源之间：26天拓宽英语阅读边界 / 边明锐，薛非主编. —北京：北京理工大学出版社，2020.4（2021.1 重印）

ISBN 978-7-5682-8399-1

Ⅰ.①题… Ⅱ.①边… ②薛… Ⅲ.①英语–阅读教学–研究生–入学考试–自学参考资料 Ⅳ.① H319.37

中国版本图书馆 CIP 数据核字（2020）第 064090 号

出版发行 / 北京理工大学出版社有限责任公司
社　　址 / 北京市海淀区中关村南大街 5 号
邮　　编 / 100081
电　　话 /（010）68914775（总编室）
　　　　　（010）82562903（教材售后服务热线）
　　　　　（010）68948351（其他图书服务热线）
网　　址 / http://www.bitpress.com.cn
经　　销 / 全国各地新华书店
印　　刷 / 三河市良远印务有限公司
开　　本 / 787 毫米 × 1092 毫米　1/16
印　　张 / 12.5　　　　　　　　　　　　　　　责任编辑 / 王晓莉
字　　数 / 312 千字　　　　　　　　　　　　　文案编辑 / 王晓莉
版　　次 / 2020 年 4 月第 1 版　2021 年 1 月第 2 次印刷　责任校对 / 刘亚男
定　　价 / 50.00 元　　　　　　　　　　　　　责任印制 / 王美丽

图书出现印装质量问题，请拨打售后服务热线，本社负责调换

前　言

题源外刊一直是考研英语备考中的重要资料，历届考生之所以愿意在百忙之中挤出宝贵的时间来学习外刊文章，主要是因为它能帮我们实现以下三个目标：

1. 完成从词句到篇章的语言能力过渡；
2. 熟悉考研英语阅读题材并积累必要的通识；
3. 预知当年的考研英语阅读话题甚至原文。

接下来笔者就围绕这三个目标简要介绍《题源之间：26天拓宽英语阅读边界》（以下简称《题源之间》）一书的相关特点：

首先，很多考生在寒假到春季开学这段时期完成词汇和长难句的学习后，都会打开考研英语阅读真题一试身手，却发现自己即便能认识文中的每个词，能分析清楚每个长难句，但在整体阅读速度以及对文章主旨的把握上还远远达不到真题的要求。这时大家就会陷入"一看基础词汇语法就懂，一读真题文章就懵"的经典 dilemma（进退两难的困境）中。为了帮大家完成从基础词句理解到真题阅读实战的过渡，笔者在挑选外刊文章时对其词汇、句法的难度进行了严格的筛查和精细的调整，全书的整体难度介于英语一和英语二之间。书中解析部分的"生词点睛"模块也并非一味地标注文章中的生词，而是突出各位考生在前期理解不到位而考研又常考的重难词；"重点表达"模块对文中地道的句式和表达进行仿写、拓写，在加强对原文句子理解的同时，便于考生学以致用；此外，每篇文章最后还设有"词意选选看"模块，方便考生进行自测。

其次，考研英语阅读真题中的文章全部选自《卫报》《大西洋月刊》《基督教科学箴言报》等西方严肃报刊以及《科学》《经济学人》这样的学术型期刊。上述文章的选材特点导致考研英语阅读除了语言难度颇高外，理解难度也非各位考生在高考、四六级中接触过的文章难度可比。其中一些文章涉及西方政治经济、法律体系、高等教育与科研系统等思辨性话题，如果考生事先对相关话题没有一定的了解和思考，即便从字面意思上"读懂"了全文，也会不明所以，这就是往届考生口中考研英语阅读"不说人话"的特点。本书从《卫报》《基督教科学箴言报》《新闻周刊》等近年最热门的题源外刊中模仿考研英语真题的偏好选取了相关文章，并整理成"人与自然""科技与反思""企业与社会""政策与民生"四大专题，希望能借助专题形式帮大家建立起全面且深刻的认识。每篇文章还设有"背景知识"模块，进行重要名词科普和通识拓展，尽可能地给大家提供相关话题的外延知识。

　　笔者相信每一位阅读题源外刊的考生，都或多或少地抱着买彩票的心理，总希望当年考研英语真题中恰好出现一篇自己读过的文章。笔者有幸押中 1 篇 2020 年考研英语一阅读真题的原文，在为本书挑选文章时我也秉承了与押题一致的标准，从 2019 年 11 月到 2020 年 3 月的文章中尽可能地模仿命题人的思路去选题。但无论如何，题源外刊每年发布的文章数以万计，各位考生只读其中的几十篇就邂逅真题的概率微乎其微。虽然命中原文的概率很低，但本书的 26 篇文章在话题上必然与 2022 年的考研英语真题有较高的重合度，对今年热点话题的深入了解一定能让诸位在考场上占尽先机。因此我恳请各位考生摒弃机会主义的想法，将有限的复习精力放在有相对稳定回报的工作上。如果真的能在今年考研的试卷上再次见到《题源之间》的文章，不妨当作锦上添花的意外收获。

　　最后，为了方便各位考生高效地使用本书，我和薛非老师为本书 26 篇文章录制了配套视频，结合大家在考研复习中的知识结构和学习难点，从词、句、篇、话题、通识等角度对文章进行了讲解。希望各位考生能充分利用《题源之间》实现上述三大目标。Bridge the gap between you and your dream!

边明锐

目 录

专题一 人与自然

第 1 天 ………………………………………………………… 003
第 2 天 ………………………………………………………… 010
第 3 天 ………………………………………………………… 018
第 4 天 ………………………………………………………… 025
第 5 天 ………………………………………………………… 031

专题二 科技与反思

第 1 天 ………………………………………………………… 039
第 2 天 ………………………………………………………… 046
第 3 天 ………………………………………………………… 053
第 4 天 ………………………………………………………… 059
第 5 天 ………………………………………………………… 065
第 6 天 ………………………………………………………… 073
第 7 天 ………………………………………………………… 082
第 8 天 ………………………………………………………… 090

专题三　企业与社会

第1天	102
第2天	109
第3天	117
第4天	124
第5天	131

专题四　政策与民生

第1天	142
第2天	148
第3天	155
第4天	161
第5天	167
第6天	173
第7天	181
第8天	188

专题一 人与自然

导　言

近年来，全球范围内各种极端气候灾害频频发生。在这种背景下，环保类题材的文章一跃成为考研阅读中的"新贵"，其考查频率不断提高，尤其是在考研英语二中，环保类题材的考查频率已经达到了每年必考一篇甚至两篇的程度。考研英语一在往年同样考过环保类话题，故 2022 年的考研，我们势必还会见到至少一篇环保类主题的文章。

除了考查频率提高外，环保类主题的文章还具备可预测性的特点：历年的环保类真题无一例外，都与当年的重大气候问题、热门环保理念、争议性环保政策直接相关。相比科技、政策、民生等话题，环保类话题是最容易做到提前预测、提前准备的，所以学习性价比很高。

同时，环保类文章有多种切入和观察角度：作者既可以聚焦"自然"这一端，客观介绍重大自然灾害的具体情况或科普自然界运作的客观规律，写成科普说明文；也可以关注环境问题中"人"的存在，探讨政府政策、企业、社会名人、普通公民在环境问题治理中的正面或负面作用，写成议论型文章，并与其他考研阅读母题形成交集。

《题源之间》将"人与自然"作为其第一专题正是基于以上的诸多考虑。本专题总共设 5 篇文章，从 2019 年以"环保公主"桑伯格为代表的环保抗议行动，到 2020 年年初震惊世界的澳洲大火，再到碳减排以及可再生能源领域的最新进展，基本涵盖了当前环保领域的主流话题。希望各位考生经过本专题的学习，能对当前世界存在的主要环保问题、主要解决思路以及在气候治理中所面临的重大挑战形成生动而具体的认识。

2010—2021 年相关考研英语阅读真题

英语一

2013　Text-1　快时尚行业之罪

2021　Text-2　扶贫项目与环境保护的关系

英语二

2016　Text-2　濒临灭绝的小草原榛鸡

2017　Text-4　野火问题的治理与反思

2018　Text-2　可再生能源的开发和利用

2019　Text-2　森林与"碳缸"

2019　Text-4　如何应对塑料危机

2020　Text-3　欧洲空气污染治理问题

第 1 天

"You are in no position to lecture the public about anything," Golden Globes host Ricky Gervais told his audience in a pointedly irreverent opening speech on Sunday. By the evening's end, following statements about the bushfires from actors including Russell Crowe and Cate Blanchett, he had apparently changed his mind—ending the evening with his own call for donations to the relief efforts. Charitable gifts will no doubt be welcomed by their recipients. But the evening's most consequential remarks were those, including Mr Crowe's and Ms Blanchett's, that firmly linked the fires to global heating—directly challenging the denialism of the Australian prime minister, Scott Morrison, who, even in the face of record temperatures and unthinkable devastation, refuses to commit his government to stronger decarbonisation measures, or withdraw his support for coal production and exports.

In an ideal world, it would probably not fall to film stars to advocate for evidence-based policies to protect the planet from catastrophe, particularly when such policies are supported by the UN and scientific institutions around the world. But while speeches and social media posts expressing sympathy for victims of this and other disasters, or promoting fundraisers and campaigns on other issues, are often and easily mocked, it makes more sense to focus on the policy failures that give rise to such efforts than to criticise pop or sports stars for their philanthropic activities, even when these appear clumsy or self-serving.

In the case of the climate emergency, the underlying failures are so grave and numerous as to remain extremely difficult for many people to take in. While denial of global heating itself is finally waning in the face of irrefutable proof, denial of the actions that are necessary to curb it is prevalent—as can be seen from the simple fact that emissions are still rising. Even as the bushfires dominate global headlines, climate-linked disasters in other parts of the world, such as a threatened famine in Zambia, or the battle for the Amazon being waged in Brazil, struggle to attract a fraction of the same attention.

Anger is a justified response to such blatant climate injustices. Particularly when many of the worst-affected poorer countries are those with the lowest historic greenhouse gas emissions, philanthropy—even if it were forthcoming—would not provide an adequate form of redress. Lasting climate solutions will require a massive reallocation of global resources, with particular emphasis on infrastructure in developing countries. Only governments and international institutions have the necessary policymaking levers.

文章大意

第一段：金球奖主持人态度1日内发生180°转变，演艺圈大腕发起慈善募捐，抨击澳大利亚政府抗灾不力。

第二段：正是政府的失位导致了原本不相干的演艺圈人士不得不为抗灾与气候问题募捐站台。故即便其不专业、有私心，也无可厚非。

第三段：当前否认主义的表现形式从否认问题的存在转变为面临问题不作为。而气候问题正以多种形式在全球爆发，愈演愈烈。

第四段：强调当前存在的"气候不公"问题，指出全球气候危机已非慈善行为能解决，需要各国政府与国际机构制定相关政策。

逐段精讲

Para. 1 "You are in no position to lecture the public about anything," **Golden Globes** host Ricky Gervais told his audience in a pointedly irreverent opening speech on Sunday. By the evening's end, following statements about the bushfires from actors including Russell Crowe and Cate Blanchett, he had apparently changed his mind—ending the evening with his own call for donations to the relief efforts. Charitable gifts will no doubt be welcomed by their recipients. But the evening's most consequential remarks were those, including Mr Crowe's and Ms Blanchett's, that firmly linked the fires to global

译文 "你们没有权力教育公众任何事情。"金球奖主持人瑞奇·热维斯周日在开幕演讲中很不客气地向他的观众们说道。而到了当天晚上，随着罗素·克劳和凯特·布兰切特等演员相继就山火问题表态，热维斯也显然改变了想法——当晚他亲自呼吁大众为赈灾工作捐款。慈善物资无疑会受到灾区接收者们的欢迎。而这还不是当晚最具影响力的言论，包含克劳先生和布兰切特女士的发言在内的诸多言论都坚定地将火灾

heating—directly challenging the denialism of the Australian prime minister, Scott Morrison, who, even in the face of record temperatures and unthinkable devastation, refuses to commit his government to stronger decarbonisation measures, or withdraw his support for coal production and exports.	与全球气候变暖联系在了一起——矛头直指澳大利亚总理斯科特·莫里森的否认主义。即使面对破纪录的高温和火灾造成的难以想象的破坏，莫里森仍然拒绝让他的政府采取更有力的碳减排措施，抑或停止对煤炭生产和出口的支持。

背景知识

Golden Globes：金球奖（Golden Globe Awards），是美国的一个电影与电视奖项，以正式晚宴的方式举行，举办方是好莱坞外国记者协会。此奖从1944年起，每年举办一次。此奖的最终结果由96位记者的投票产生。

生词点睛

lecture v. 指责，训斥	**pointedly** adv. 尖锐地；明显地
irreverent adj. 不尊敬的	**bushfire** n. 山火；林火
relief effort 救济工作	**recipient** n. 接收者
consequential adj. 有影响力的；作为结果的	**denialism** n. 否认主义
prime minister 首相；总理	**decarbonisation** n. 碳减排

重点表达

❖ be in no position to do sth. 无权做某事

I **am in no position to** comment on the matter. 我无权就此事发表评论。

❖ link A to/with B 将 A 与 B（从逻辑上）关联起来

The scholars have **linked** the crime rate **to** social circumstances. 学者们认为犯罪率与社会环境有关。

❖ commit sb. to sth. 使某人致力于某事

The achievement of your goal is assured when you **commit** yourself **to** it. 当你全身心投入时，你的目标就注定会实现。

Para. 2 In an ideal world, it would probably not fall to film stars to advocate for evidence-based policies to protect the planet from catastrophe, particularly when such policies are supported by the **UN** and scientific institutions around the world. But while speeches and social media posts expressing sympathy for victims of this and other disasters, or promoting fundraisers and campaigns on other issues, are often and easily mocked, it makes more sense to focus on the policy failures that give rise to such efforts than to criticise pop or sports stars for their philanthropic activities, even when these appear clumsy or self-serving.

译文 理想情况下，可能根本无须影视明星为这种保护地球免受灾害的务实政策站台，更何况这些政策背后还有联合国和全世界科研机构的支持。然而各类演讲和社交媒体文章在向这次和其他灾难的受害者表达同情或为其他问题筹集善款并开展活动时，经常遭到嘲讽，我们更应该关注的是催生以上现象的政策问题本身，而不是去批评进行慈善活动的娱乐和体育明星，哪怕这些慈善活动有些不得当或意在谋取私利。

背景知识

UN：联合国（United Nations）是第二次世界大战后成立的国际组织，是一个由主权国家组成的国际组织。1945年10月24日，在美国旧金山签订生效的《联合国宪章》标志着联合国正式成立。联合国致力于促进各国在国际法、国际安全、经济发展、社会进步、人权及实现世界和平方面的合作。

生词点睛

advocate for 呼吁；提倡	**post** *n.* 邮件
fundraiser *n.* 募捐活动；募捐者	**mock** *v.* 嘲笑
philanthropic *adj.* 慈善的	**clumsy** *adj.* 笨拙的；蹩脚的

重点表达

❖ in an ideal world 理想情况下

In an ideal world, each of us would have a considerate caregiver to meet our physical and emotional needs as we age. 理想情况下，当我们老了，每个人都会有一个体贴的护工来照顾我们的身心需求。

- **fall to sb.** (某种责任、义务）落在了某人肩上

In the traditional idea, much of the responsibility for a date **falls to** the man. 传统观念中，男方应该在约会时采取主动。

- **it makes sense to do sth.** 做某事是明智 / 合理 / 应该的

It makes sense to eat a reasonably balanced diet when slimming. 在减肥过程中应该保持膳食的合理均衡。

Para. 3 In the case of the climate emergency, the underlying failures are so grave and numerous as to remain extremely difficult for many people to take in. While denial of global heating itself is finally waning in the face of irrefutable proof, denial of the actions that are necessary to curb it is prevalent—as can be seen from the simple fact that emissions are still rising. Even as the bushfires dominate global headlines, climate-linked disasters in other parts of the world, such as a threatened famine in Zambia, or the battle for the **Amazon** being waged in Brazil, struggle to attract a fraction of the same attention.

译文 在当前的气候危机之下潜藏着大量严重的问题，大部分人都难以厘清其中的头绪。在无可辩驳的证据面前，否认全球气候变暖现象存在的声音逐渐消失了；然而拒绝采取必要行动来阻止气候变暖的情况却非常普遍——这点从碳排放如今仍然在攀升这一简单的事实中就可见一斑。就在澳大利亚山火占据了全球媒体头条的同时，世界其他地区的气候灾难也在争取获得人们的一些关注，如赞比亚的饥荒危机以及巴西发起的保卫亚马孙森林运动。

背景知识

Amazon： 亚马孙雨林位于南美洲亚马孙平原，总面积550万平方公里，占世界雨林总面积的一半。这片雨林横跨8个南美国家，其中60%位于巴西境内。2019年，亚马孙森林火灾频发，其中，巴西、秘鲁与玻利维亚交界处的亚马孙地区为火灾重灾区。

生词点睛

underlying *adj.* 潜在的；根源的	**grave** *adj.* 严重的
numerous *adj.* 不计其数的	**take in** 理解
wane *v.* 衰落；减弱	**curb** *v.* 阻碍；阻止
prevalent *adj.* 普遍的；盛行的	**wage** *v.* 发起；发动

重点表达

❖ in the face of irrefutable proof 在无可辩驳的证据面前
In the face of irrefutable proof, the defendant finally caved in and pleaded guilty. 面对如山的铁证，被告最终俯首认罪。

❖ dominate headlines 某事占据了各大媒体的头版
The fuel crisis continues to **dominate headlines**. 燃料危机一直是头版要闻。

拓 dominate Wechat Moments 某事在微信朋友圈刷屏了
Kobe's passing **dominates Wechat Moments**. 科比的离世在朋友圈刷屏了。

Para. 4 Anger is a justified response to such blatant climate injustices. Particularly when many of the worst-affected poorer countries are those with the lowest historic greenhouse gas emissions, philanthropy—even if it were forthcoming—would not provide an adequate form of redress. Lasting climate solutions will require a massive reallocation of global resources, with particular emphasis on infrastructure in developing countries. Only governments and international institutions have the necessary policymaking levers.

译文 面对如此明显的气候方面的不公，感到愤怒是理所应当的。很多温室气体历史排放量最少的贫穷国家恰恰是受灾最严重的地方，这种情况下即便慈善物资能马上到位，也不足以补偿它们的损失。对全球资源进行大规模的再分配才是解决气候问题的长久之计，其中尤其需要重视发展中国家的基础设施建设。只有各国政府和国际机构掌握着落实上述措施所必需的政策工具。

生词点睛

justified *adj.* 正当的；合乎情理的	**blatant** *adj.* 明目张胆的；公然的
injustice *n.* 不公正	**redress** *n.* 补偿；赔偿
reallocation *n.* 再分配	**infrastructure** *n.* 基础设施
policymaking *n.* 政策制定；决策	**lever** *n.* 工具；杠杆，操纵杆

重点表达

❖ **lasting solution** 长久之计，永久的解决方案

Eurozone countries have made progress but much more needs to be done to reach a **lasting solution**. 欧元区的国家已经取得了一些进展，但离彻底解决这一问题还有很长的路要走。

❖ **with particular emphasis on sth.** 尤其重视/针对某事

These Apps are optimized for use on mobile devices, **with particular emphasis on** the iPhone and Android platforms. 这些应用已针对移动设备上的使用做了优化，尤其是iPhone和安卓平台。

词意选选看

1. remark ____　　　　　　　a. 严重的
2. consequential ____　　　　b. 碳减排
3. decarbonisation ____　　　c. 基础设施
4. mock ____　　　　　　　　d. 言论
5. clumsy ____　　　　　　　e. 有影响力的
6. curb ____　　　　　　　　f. 正当的
7. grave ____　　　　　　　　g. 嘲笑
8. reallocation ____　　　　　h. 阻碍；阻止
9. infrastructure ____　　　　i. 笨拙的
10. justified ____　　　　　　j. 再分配

拓展阅读

否认主义

　　In the psychology of human behavior, denialism is a person's choice to deny reality as a way to avoid a psychologically uncomfortable truth. Denialism is an essentially irrational action that withholds the validation of a historical experience or event, when a person refuses to accept an empirically verifiable reality.

延伸思考：否认主义行为的来源是什么？其危害有哪些？

第 2 天

Oxfam has calculated that carbon emissions produced by the world's wealthiest 10% are equivalent to those of the poorest half. Today, we publish new research showing that the average Brit will emit more carbon in first two weeks of 2020 than the citizens of seven African nations emit in an entire year.

The good news is that there are increasing signs that the public is ready to act. As many as four in five Britons said they are likely to take one of a number of actions this year to reduce their carbon footprint. More than two-thirds (68%) said they were likely to use energy-efficient products or utility providers and 79% of people said they were likely to recycle more. In September, tens of thousands of people took Oxfam's SecondHandSeptember pledge not to buy new clothes for a month, saving carbon equivalent to driving round the world 200 times.

But people also need help to adapt. Six out of 10 people in Britain want the government to do more to tackle climate change and solutions are available—improving public transport, introducing schemes to make greener homes more affordable or tax incentives to encourage lower-carbon lifestyles.

There are no shortcuts—we can't argue our way out of the climate emergency by using statistical tricks or clever rhetoric. Greta Thunberg has accused the UK of "very creative carbon accounting", because our official figures exclude "imported" emissions from goods and services we use that are produced outside our borders, such as electronic goods made in Asia or overseas flights. Climate crisis doesn't end at our coastline: our shared, international targets on climate action are called "global goals" for good reason and government policy needs to account for that fact.

We, and other wealthy industrialised nations like us, have been responsible for the majority of emissions over the past century and a half and therefore have a responsibility to support poorer nations in reducing their own emissions and adapting to the brutal impacts of a climate crisis they did little to cause. Expecting that we can simply "offset" our carbon emissions through schemes overseas, such as paying poorer countries to grow forests instead of food, risks pushing people already on the frontline of climate crisis even deeper into hunger and poverty.

Wealthy nations have pledged to provide $100bn (£89bn) in climate finance every year by

2020. The UK should use its position as host of this year's climate talks to push other countries to follow its lead in helping to reach this target and beyond while ensuring that funding doesn't come from cuts to medicines, schools and other overseas aid commitments.

文章大意

第一、二段：严峻的气候危机和相关统计数据让英国普通民众意识到自己环保减排的责任，人们准备采取各种减排行动。

第三段：要想促成民众的环保行动，政府政策的引导必不可少。

第四、五段：气候危机具有全球性，所以地方保护主义思维不可取；同时，英国作为过去一个多世纪的碳排放大户，将减排工作推给贫穷国家的做法也不道德。

第六段：英国应该积极利用其全球影响力致力于解决环境问题，向海外国家提供实打实的援助。

逐段精讲

Para. 1 Oxfam has calculated that carbon emissions produced by the world's wealthiest 10% are equivalent to those of the poorest half. Today, we publish new research showing that the average Brit will emit more carbon in first two weeks of 2020 than the citizens of seven African nations emit in an entire year.

译文 根据乐施会的计算，世界上最富裕的10%人口与最贫穷的50%人口的二氧化碳排放量是相当的。如今我们新发布的研究表明，普通英国民众在2020年前两个星期里排放的二氧化碳比7个非洲国家的居民一整年排放的还要多。

背景知识

Oxfam：乐施会（原名 Oxford Committee for Famine Relief）是一个具有国际影响力的发展和救援组织的联盟，由十三个独立运作的乐施会成员组成。"助人自助，对抗贫穷"是乐施会的宗旨和目标。

生词点睛

average *adj.* 普通的；典型的	**Brit** *n.* 英国人（Briton 的缩写）
citizen *n.* 市民；公民	**entire** *adj.* 整个的；完全的

重点表达

❖ be equivalent to 等同于；等价于
One kilometer **is equivalent to** two li. 一公里等于两华里。
Changing his position **is equivalent to** giving him the sack. 调换他的工作岗位等于是解雇了他。

Para. 2 The good news is that there are increasing signs that the public is ready to act. As many as four in five Britons said they are likely to take one of a number of actions this year to reduce their carbon footprint. More than two-thirds (68%) said they were likely to use energy-efficient products or utility providers and 79% of people said they were likely to recycle more. In September, tens of thousands of people took Oxfam's SecondHandSeptember pledge not to buy new clothes for a month, saving carbon equivalent to driving round the world 200 times.

译文 好消息是，越来越多的迹象表明公众已经准备采取行动。五分之四的英国人表示他们今年很可能会采取一定的措施来减少自己的碳排放量。超过三分之二（68%）的人表示自己会使用节能的产品或能源供应商，79% 的人表示可能会进行更多的回收再利用。9 月份，成千上万的人响应乐施会的"二手九月"活动，发誓一个月内不买新衣服，由此减少的碳排放量与驾车环游世界 200 次相当。

生词点睛

four in five 五分之四的	**be likely to do** 很可能做某事
carbon footprint 碳排放量	**energy-efficient** *adj.* 高效能的；节能的
utility *n.* 效用；公用事业	**pledge** *n.* 保证；承诺；誓言

重点表达

❖ there are increasing signs that... 越来越多的迹象表明……

There are increasing signs that the subject is starting to get the attention it deserves. 越来越多的迹象表明,这一问题已逐渐得到应有的重视。

❖ tens of thousands of 成千上万的;数以万计的

The new job bill would put **tens of thousands of** teachers back to work across the country, and modernize at least 35, 000 schools. 新的就业法案将会使全国成千上万的教师重返工作岗位,并对至少 35 000 所学校进行现代化改造。

拓 tens of millions of 数千万的

Tens of millions of migrants who work far afield and flock home for the Chinese new year are being priced out the rail market and have to go by bus. 数千万在外打工的农民工在春节返乡时由于买不起火车票而不得不坐大巴。

Para. 3 But people also need help to adapt. Six out of 10 people in Britain want the government to do more to tackle climate change and solutions are available—improving public transport, introducing schemes to make greener homes more affordable or tax incentives to encourage lower-carbon lifestyles.

译文 但人们也需要外界的帮助来调整和适应。六成的英国人希望政府能采取更多的行动来应对气候变化问题,解决方案是现成的——改善公共交通,引入政策以使环保住房更便宜,或通过税收激励手段来鼓励低碳生活。

生词点睛

tackle v. 处理;应对	**transport** n. 交通
scheme n. 计划,方案;阴谋,诡计	**incentive** n. 激励;刺激

重点表达

❖ six out of 10 十分之六的

Between the 2001 and 2009 surveys, **six out of 10** of alumni secured a more senior job following their MBA. 在2001年至2009年的调查期间,六成学员在读完MBA后得到了更高的职位。

❖ **make sth. more affordable for sb.** 使某人买得起某物

The government will work to **make** high-quality medical resources **more affordable** and accessible **for** all the citizens. 政府将努力让所有公民都负担得起并享受得到高质量的医疗资源。

Para. 4 There are no shortcuts—we can't argue our way out of the climate emergency by using statistical tricks or clever rhetoric. **Greta Thunberg** has accused the UK of "very creative carbon accounting", because our official figures exclude "imported" emissions from goods and services we use that are produced outside our borders, such as electronic goods made in Asia or overseas flights. Climate crisis doesn't end at our coastline: our shared, international targets on climate action are called "global goals" for good reason and government policy needs to account for that fact.

译文 解决气候问题没有捷径可走——我们无法通过统计学把戏或巧言辞令来走出气候危机。格蕾塔·桑伯格指控英国使用了"非常具有创造力的碳排放统计方式",因为我们的官方统计中把"进口的"碳排放排除在外,这些碳排放源自国人使用但在国外生产的商品和服务,如亚洲制造的电子产品或国际航班。但气候危机不会止于英国的海岸线:我们在气候行动上共同的国际目标之所以被称作"全球目标"是有其道理的,我们的政府政策中需要体现这一点。

背景知识

Greta Thunberg:格蕾塔·桑伯格,瑞典青年活动人士、激进环保分子,曾在联合国气候行动峰会上当面指责各国政要在环保气候问题上的不作为。2019年获诺贝尔和平奖的提名,并当选《时代》周刊年度人物。

生词点睛

shortcut *n.* 捷径	**statistical** *adj.* 统计学的
trick *n.* 把戏;诡计	**rhetoric** *n.* 修辞;华而不实的语言
exclude *v.* 排除	**goods** *n.* 货物;商品
border *n.* 国界	**for good reason** 出于充足的理由

重点表达

❖ **accuse** sb. **of** sth. 指控 / 指责某人做了某事

Don't **accuse** people **of** doing something if you don't have any evidence. 在没有证据的情况下不要随意指控他人。

❖ **account for** ① 解释，说明，导致 ② 负责 ③ 占

These reasons largely **account for** the American Civil War. 以上原因很大程度上导致了美国内战（解释了美国内战的发生）。

Ministers should **account for** their indecision. 部长们需要为自己决策上的优柔寡断负责。

The minority nationalities **account for** 6% of the population. 少数民族占总人口的 6%。

Para. 5 We, and other wealthy industrialised nations like us, have been responsible for the majority of emissions over the past century and a half and therefore have a responsibility to support poorer nations in reducing their own emissions and adapting to the brutal impacts of a climate crisis they did little to cause. Expecting that we can simply "offset" our carbon emissions through schemes overseas, such as paying poorer countries to grow forests instead of food, risks pushing people already on the frontline of climate crisis even deeper into hunger and poverty.

译文 英国以及其他像英国一样富裕的工业化国家造成了过去一百五十年里的大部分碳排放，因此我们有责任帮助那些相对贫穷的国家减排，并助其应对气候危机带来的猛烈冲击，这些国家并非罪魁祸首，但承担了气候危机的恶果。指望着通过掏钱让贫穷国家不种粮食而是去种树的这类海外政策来"抵消"我们以前的碳排放，会将原本就处在气候危机一线的人们置于更严重的饥饿与贫穷的危险中。

生词点睛

industrialised adj. 工业化的	**brutal** adj. 兽性的；野蛮的；冷酷的
offset v. 抵消	**risk** v. 冒着……的风险；将……置于危险中

重点表达

❖ **be responsible for** 对……负有责任

As the former chancellor of the exchequer, he **is responsible for** much of this financial chaos. 作为前财政大臣，他对当前的财政混乱负有不可推卸的责任。

Para. 6 Wealthy nations have pledged to provide $100bn (£89bn) in climate finance every year by 2020. The UK should use its position as host of this year's **climate talks** to push other countries to follow its lead in helping to reach this target and beyond while ensuring that funding doesn't come from cuts to medicines, schools and other overseas aid commitments.

译文 富裕国家已承诺自2020年起，每年针对气候问题提供1 000亿美元（合890亿英镑）的资金。英国应该利用其今年的气候会议主办国地位来推动其他国家效仿自己的做法，以实现甚至超额完成原定目标；同时还应保证这笔资金不以削减医疗、教育以及其他海外援助承诺的资金为代价。

背景知识

2020 UN climate talks：2020年联合国气候变化会议，也称为COP26，是第26届联合国气候变化会议，计划于2020年11月9日至19日在英国政府的主持下于苏格兰的格拉斯哥举行，被认为是自2015年签署巴黎气候协议以来最重要的气候变化会议。

生词点睛

| finance n. 财政资助 | commitment n. 承诺 |

重点表达

❖ follow one's lead 效仿某人；以某人为榜样

The government is likely to **follow the lead of** California's Stanford University, which created the high-tech cluster now known as Silicon Valley. 政府很可能会效仿加州斯坦福大学，再造一个像硅谷那样高科技企业扎堆的地方。

· 词意选选看 ·

1. equivalent ____   a. 处理；应对

2. utility _____   b. 保证；承诺

3. pledge _____   c. 相等的，相同的

4. tackle _____   d. 排除

5. transport _____   e. 效用；公共事业

6. scheme _____   f. 抵消

7. incentive _____   g. 交通

8. exclude _____   h. 承诺

9. offset _____   i. 计划，方案

10. commitment _____   j. 激励；刺激

拓展阅读

绿色经济学

Green economics focuses on the importance of the health of the biosphere to human well-being. Consequently, most Greens distrust conventional capitalism, as it tends to emphasize economic growth while ignoring ecological health; the "full cost" of economic growth often includes damage to the biosphere, which is unacceptable according to green politics. Green economics considers such growth to be "uneconomic growth"—material increase that nonetheless lowers overall quality of life.

延伸思考： 全球化与地方保护主义在气候危机中扮演了怎样的角色？

第 3 天

The biggest story in climate in 2019 is the way in which climate activism has finally broken through. It seems obvious in retrospect that the kids were the key. Self-organised, serious and frank about their anger at seeing their futures contaminated by politicians who won't even live to see the consequences, they have lent a powerful moral drive to the entire movement.

Climate protests are not new, but they acquired a new urgency this year. It has been encouraged by immediate effects of the climate crisis: deadly heatwaves across Europe, wildfires in the US, cyclones in the Pacific and record-breaking high temperatures across the world. For several years scientists have been speaking in more concrete terms about the consequences of climate change, and have been willing to connect it directly to current events. The link between the climate emergency and our own lives has never seemed clearer. Finally, after decades of activists struggling to push the crisis into the larger consciousness, poll after poll shows that public concern, and desire for action, is at an all-time high.

The question that became clearer as the year went on was, having achieved what the climate movement always wanted—prominent and positive media coverage, widespread public support, audiences with world leaders—was it possible to effect any actual political change? The spectacle of Thunberg arriving at international meetings and parliaments and accusing heads of state of hypocrisy to their faces is undoubtedly thrilling. But climate politics itself still seems far from any genuine watershed moment.

There has been little concrete progress. What the protests have sparked, instead, is a rush by governments to declare a "climate emergency" and to set future emissions targets. In previous years this alone would have seemed radical enough; now, however, the gap between words and actions has widened too far, and credulity is in short supply. The climate researcher Rebecca Willis put the new standard scornfully earlier this month: "Targets don't reduce carbon. Policies do."

There has been some hope on that front. Politicians in the UK and the US took on comprehensive climate policies for the first time. These either directly or indirectly reference the concept of a "green new deal"—pairing increased spending on climate with a larger social transformation, and breaking down the wall that separates climate policy from the rest of national politics. But crucially, nothing similar has been brought forward by a government actually in power.

专题一　人与自然

文章大意

第一段：2019年环保主义运动取得了重大突破，孩子们才是推动环保运动的主力军。

第二段：环保问题今年变得异常严重，这使得环保抗议取得了显著的效果。

第三段：虽然今年环保人士出尽风头，但仍未促成任何重大环保政策的出台。

第四段：面对抗议声，政府只是做了些制定减排目标的表面文章。然而解决环保问题需要的是具体可行的政策。

第五段：最近英美政府采取的综合性环保政策让我们看到了一丝希望，政府需要综合运用多方面的政策来解决环保问题。

逐段精讲

Para. 1 The biggest story in climate in 2019 is the way in which climate activism has finally broken through. It seems obvious in retrospect that the kids were the key. Self-organised, serious and frank about their anger at seeing their futures contaminated by politicians who won't even live to see the consequences, they have lent a powerful moral drive to the entire movement.

译文 2019年环境方面最大的新闻是激进环保主义最终取得突破的方式。事后看来答案似乎很明显，孩子们才是关键。当发现自己的未来正被政客们污染，而政客们甚至在有生之年都无法见证自己播种的恶果时，自发、认真而且能坦诚表达自己愤怒的孩子们给整个环保运动带来了道德层面上的驱动力。

生词点睛

| activism *n*. 激进主义；行动主义 | retrospect *n*. 回顾 |
| self-organised *adj*. 自组织的；自发的 | contaminate *v*. 污染；玷污 |

重点表达

❖ break through 取得突破

I broke through the poverty barrier and it was education that did it. 我摆脱了贫困，这要归功于教育。

Para. 2 Climate protests are not new, but they acquired a new urgency this year. It has been encouraged by the obvious immediate effects of the climate crisis: deadly heatwaves across Europe, wildfires in the US, cyclones in the Pacific and record-breaking high temperatures across the world. For several years scientists have been speaking in more concrete terms about the consequences of climate change, and have been willing to connect it directly to current events. The link between the climate emergency and our own lives has never seemed clearer. Finally, after decades of activists struggling to push the crisis into the larger consciousness, poll after poll shows that public concern, and desire for action, is at an all-time high.

译文 环保抗议并非什么新鲜事，但今年显得尤为紧要。席卷欧洲的致命热浪、美国的森林大火、太平洋飓风、世界范围内破纪录的高温，诸多气候危机带来的直观影响助长了抗议之声。多年以来，科学家们对气候变化带来的后果描述得越发具体了，他们一直想把气候变化与眼下的种种灾难直接关联起来。气候危机与人类生存生活之间的关系从未像现在这般清晰。最终，经过激进的环保主义者几十年来对气候危机的奔走相告，一份份民调显示，当前公众对气候问题的担忧以及对其应对措施的渴望都达到了历史最高点。

生词点睛

protest n. 抗议	**cyclone** n. 飓风；旋风
record-breaking adj. 破纪录的	**term** n. 词语；术语
consciousness n. 意识；认知	**poll** n. 民意调查

重点表达

❖ be at an all-time high 达到了历史最高点；创历史新高
Attendances at football matches **are at an all-time high**. 观看足球比赛的人数达到了历史最高纪录。

Para. 3 The question that became clearer as the year went on was, having achieved what the climate movement always wanted—prominent and positive media coverage, widespread public support, audiences with world leaders—was it possible to effect any actual political change? The spectacle of Thunberg arriving at international meetings and parliaments and accusing heads of state of hypocrisy to their faces is undoubtedly thrilling. But climate politics itself still seems far from any genuine watershed moment.

译文 今年以来越发明显的一个问题是，在环保运动终于得偿所愿，得到了大量积极的媒体宣传、广泛的公众支持以及包括各国领导人在内的听众后，它是否真的能促成一些实质性的政治变革呢？桑伯格在国际性会议以及议会上大出风头，她当面指责各国领导人虚伪的场面无疑是激动人心的。但真正具有转折意义的气候政治运动似乎仍然遥不可及。

生词点睛

prominent adj. 显眼的；突出的	**coverage** n. 新闻报道；覆盖面
spectacle n. 壮观场面	**parliament** n. 议会
hypocrisy n. 虚伪	**thrilling** adj. 激动人心的；惊险的
genuine adj. 真正的	**watershed** n. 转折点；分水岭

重点表达

❖ to one's face 当面

He felt uncomfortable because of being criticized **to his face**. 被当面批评了两句，他就抹不开脸了。

Para. 4 There has been little concrete progress. What the protests have sparked, instead, is a rush by governments to declare a "climate emergency" and to set future emissions targets. In previous years this alone would have seemed radical enough; now, however, the gap between

译文 我们取得的实际进步少得可怜，各种抗议换来的只是政府匆忙地宣布进入"气候紧急状态"并制定未来的减排目标而已。放到早些年来看，光是这些行动就显得足够激进了；然而当今政府言行之间的落差实在太大了，导致

words and actions has widened too far, and credulity is in short supply. The climate researcher Rebecca Willis put the new standard scornfully earlier this month: "Targets don't reduce carbon. Policies do."

民众不会轻信。本月早些时候，气候学者黎贝卡·威利斯不无讽刺地评论了政府出台的新标准："目标本身无法减排，减排需要具体政策。"

生词点睛

spark v. 引发；触发	**rush** n. 匆忙；仓促的行为
radical adj. 激进的；彻底的	**credulity** n. 轻信

Para. 5 There has been some hope on that front. Politicians in the UK and the US took on comprehensive climate policies for the first time. These either directly or indirectly reference the concept of a **"green new deal"**—pairing increased spending on climate with a larger social transformation, and breaking down the wall that separates climate policy from the rest of national politics. But crucially, nothing similar has been brought forward by a government actually in power.

译文 这方面还是有些希望的。英国和美国的政客们破天荒地采取了综合性的环保政策。这些政策直接或间接地参考了"绿色新政"的理念——在增加气候治理资金投入的同时进行更广泛的社会转型，打破将气候政策与其他国家政策割裂的思考模式。但重要的是，目前为止任何一个实际掌权的政府都没有做过类似的事情。

背景知识

green new deal："绿色新政"是由联合国前秘书长潘基文在 2008 年联合国气候变化大会上提出的一个概念，是对环境友好型政策的统称，主要涉及环境保护、污染防治、节能减排、气候变化等与人和自然的可持续发展相关的重大问题。

生词点睛

reference v. 参考；查阅	**social transformation** 社会转型
crucially adv. 至关重要地	

重点表达

❖ take on 采取；承担

No other organisation was able or willing to **take on** the job. 没有任何别的组织有能力或愿意承担此项工作。

词意选选看

1. retrospect ____
2. contaminate ____
3. protest ____
4. consciousness ____
5. poll ____
6. prominent ____
7. genuine ____
8. spark ____
9. rush ____
10. radical ____

a. 抗议
b. 真正的
c. 匆忙
d. 污染
e. 回顾
f. 意识
g. 显眼的
h. 激进的
i. 民调
j. 引发

拓展阅读

全球经济面临的困难

The global economy faces multiple, linked crises. It is a combination of accelerating climate breakdown driven by fossil fuel use, corrosive inequality, and debt-fueled over-consumption by a global minority pushing us beyond planetary ecological boundaries. These overlapping factors threaten to develop into a perfect storm making social collapse highly likely. Green New Deal helps prevent this from happening, and to lay the foundations of the economic systems of the future.

延伸思考：为什么国际社会需要从经济角度解决环境保护问题？

第 4 天

Trying to remove heat-trapping gases from Earth's atmosphere to halt global warming is a huge undertaking. But big challenges can provoke big solutions. A recent proposal even suggested one of the most radical ideas so far: Forget about reducing carbon dioxide. Instead, just push Earth's orbit 50% farther out from the sun, about where Mars is and where solar heating would be less intense. Problem solved.

A big idea no doubt, but hardly practical. Meanwhile two much more down-to-earth big ideas to cut global warming are gaining momentum. Pulling carbon dioxide from the atmosphere into the soil through reforestation and improved farming techniques could be a powerful duo. Neither idea is new, but the thinking about how to carry out these concepts keeps being refined as more research is done.

Farming techniques such as rotating crops, not turning soil over when planting, and using cover crops to restore soil quality help whatever is planted do what it does naturally: take carbon dioxide from the air and fix it in the soil. A nonprofit research group has forecast that, in theory, 100% of today's worldwide carbon emissions could be captured this way.

Among the challenges standing in the way is the need to give farmers a financial incentive to change their methods. That likely means funding the effort through carbon offsets—creating a market where carbon-emitting industries must pay to have farmers fix carbon in soils. It also means finding ways to measure how much carbon is actually being captured so its value can be established.

Preserving forested land around the world has long been seen as an important climate-saving technique. Trees also suck carbon dioxide out of the air and store it in the ground. Efforts to combat further deforestation as well as reforest degraded land are crucial. Letting degraded land naturally return to forest, rather than replanting trees, may often be the best way to go. That lets nature choose the species that will flourish in that particular region.

Changing farming techniques and regrowing forests to take carbon dioxide out of the air can't replace efforts to cut emissions. Reducing the use of fossil fuels through techniques such as generating more energy from sun and wind remains crucial. But these two approaches do show that the campaign against global warming needs to take place on many fronts, from lowering the amount of carbon dioxide going into the atmosphere to pulling more back out of it.

题源之间：**26**天拓宽英语阅读边界

文章大意

第一段：针对气候变暖问题的解决方案层出不穷，甚至有人提出通过改变轨道来使地球远离太阳。

第二段：其中有两个相对实际的办法：将空气中的二氧化碳提取出来，通过造林注入土壤中；改善农业技术。

第三、四段：新的农业技术有助于将空气中的二氧化碳锁入土壤中。但其中的一大挑战是需要通过碳补偿给农民足够的财政激励以改变其耕作方式。

第五段：减少森林的砍伐并加强植树造林也非常重要。

第六段：虽然上述做法无法完全代替节能减排的作用，但也同样不可或缺。对抗全球变暖需要双管齐下。

逐段精讲

Para. 1 Trying to remove heat-trapping gases from Earth's atmosphere to halt global warming is a huge undertaking. But big challenges can provoke big solutions. A recent proposal even suggested one of the most radical ideas so far: Forget about reducing carbon dioxide. Instead, just push Earth's orbit 50% farther out from the sun, about where Mars is and where solar heating would be less intense. Problem solved.

译文 试图通过消除地球大气中的温室气体来阻止全球气候变暖是个艰巨的任务。但重大的挑战也能带来了不起的解决方案。最近甚至有人提出了迄今为止最为激进的建议之一：别去纠结碳减排了。相反，我们只需把地球的运转轨道推远50%，大概到火星的位置，远离了太阳，热量就没那么高了。问题解决。

生词点睛

| heat-trapping *adj.* 吸热的；聚热的 | halt *v.* 阻止 |
| provoke *v.* 激起；引发 | orbit *n.* 轨道 |

Para. 2 A big idea no doubt, but hardly practical. Meanwhile two much more down-to-earth big ideas to cut global warming are gaining momentum. Pulling carbon dioxide from the atmosphere into the soil through reforestation and improved farming techniques could be a powerful duo. Neither idea is new, but the thinking about how to carry out these concepts keeps being refined as more research is done.

译文 这无疑是个大胆的想法，但实在谈不上可行。与此同时，两个更加实际的阻止气候变暖的设想在不断获得人们的支持。通过再造林将大气中的二氧化碳注入土壤与改进农业技术可以形成有力的组合。这两个设想本身并不新鲜，但关于如何落实这些设想的思考一直伴随着相关研究而不断深入。

生词点睛

practical *adj.* 可行的	down-to-earth *adj.* 务实的；现实的
momentum *n.* 动力；势头	reforestation *n.* 重新造林
duo *n.* 搭档	refine *v.* 提炼；改进

重点表达

❖ gain momentum 势头增强

Globalization continues to **gain momentum** following a slowdown after the 2008–2009 worldwide economic downturn. 全球化进程虽然受到2008—2009年全球经济低迷的影响，但此后势头又不断增强。

Para. 3 Farming techniques such as rotating crops, not turning soil over when planting, and using cover crops to restore soil quality help whatever is planted do what it does naturally: take carbon dioxide from the air and fix it in the soil. A nonprofit research group has forecast that, in theory, 100% of today's worldwide carbon emissions could be captured this way.

译文 诸如农作物轮作、不翻土种植，以及利用覆盖作物改善土壤质量等农业技术有助于各种作物实现其自然机理：从空气中吸收二氧化碳，并将其锁入土壤之中。据某个非营利研究组织预测，当今世界上100%的碳排放在理论上都可以通过上述方式来捕捉。

生词点睛

rotate *v.* 旋转；轮换	**soil** *n.* 土壤
nonprofit *adj.* 非营利的	

重点表达

❖ in theory 理论上

A school dental service exists **in theory**, but in practice, there are few dentists to work in it. 照理说，学校也有牙医诊所，可实际上，里面的牙医寥寥无几。

Para. 4 Among the challenges standing in the way is the need to give farmers a financial incentive to change their methods. That likely means funding the effort through carbon offsets—creating a market where carbon-emitting industries must pay to have farmers fix carbon in soils. It also means finding ways to measure how much carbon is actually being captured so its value can be established.

译文 当前最大的挑战是我们需要给农民们一定的财政激励以改变他们的耕作方式。这意味着我们很可能需要通过碳补偿的形式来实现它，所谓碳补偿就是创造一个交易市场，碳排放企业必须通过这个市场付钱给农民来让农民将二氧化碳锁入土壤中。这还意味着我们需要找到衡量碳捕捉量的方法，这样才能对其进行定价。

生词点睛

offset *n.* 抵消；补偿

重点表达

❖ stand in the way of sth. 阻碍某事

We cannot allow dogmatism to **stand in the way of** progress. 我们不能允许教条主义阻碍进步。

Para. 5 Preserving forested lands around the world has long been seen as an important climate-saving technique. Trees also suck carbon dioxide out of the air and store it in the ground. Efforts to combat further deforestation as well as reforest degraded land are crucial. Letting degraded land naturally return to forest, rather than replanting trees, may often be the best way to go. That lets nature choose the species that will flourish in that particular region.

译文 保护全球林地一直都被视为一项重要的环保措施。树木也能起到从空气中吸收二氧化碳并将其存入土壤的作用。努力进一步遏制滥伐森林并在退化的土地上重新造林是非常重要的。让已退化的土地自然地变回森林而非人为植树可能才是最好的办法。因为这使大自然可以选择那些能在某个特定地区繁衍生息的物种。

生词点睛

suck *v.* 吸	**combat** *v.* 防止；对抗
deforestation *n.* 滥伐森林	**degrade** *v.* 使退化；分解
flourish *v.* 茁壮成长；繁荣	**region** *n.* 地区

Para. 6 Changing farming techniques and regrowing forests to take carbon dioxide out of the air can't replace efforts to cut emissions. Reducing the use of fossil fuels through techniques such as generating more energy from sun and wind remains crucial. But these two approaches do show that the campaign against global warming needs to take place on many fronts, from lowering the amount of carbon dioxide going into the atmosphere to pulling more back out of it.

译文 改变农业技术和再造林以从空气中吸收二氧化碳的方法无法取代减排措施。通过产生更多太阳能与风能等措施来减少化石燃料的使用仍然是极为重要的。但上述的两种途径也确实说明，从减少大气中的二氧化碳排放量到尽可能多地回收二氧化碳，我们需要从多方面下手来对抗全球气候变暖。

生词点睛

replace *v.* 替代	**fossil fuel** 化石燃料

重点表达

❖ take place 发生；举行

A total solar eclipse is due to **take place** sometime tomorrow. 明天某个时刻会发生日全食。

The meeting will **take place** as planned. 会议将按预定的计划进行。

词意选选看

1. halt ____
2. provoke ____
3. practical ____
4. refine ____
5. rotate ____
6. soil ____
7. degrade ____
8. flourish ____
9. region ____
10. replace ____

a. 土壤
b. 可行的
c. 茁壮成长
d. 阻止
e. 地区
f. 激起
g. 替代
h. 旋转
i. 改进
j. 使退化

拓展阅读

碳补偿

A carbon offset is a reduction in emissions of carbon dioxide or other greenhouse gases made in order to compensate for emissions made elsewhere. Companies, governments, or other entities buy carbon offsets in order to comply with caps on the total amount of carbon dioxide they are allowed to emit.

延伸思考：碳补偿政策与其他节能减排措施在本质上有何异同？

第 5 天

The government's decision to overturn an effective five-year-old ban on new onshore wind power generation is hugely welcome. Wind provides the cheapest energy, and onshore wind is even cheaper. Onshore wind is even cheaper. It is also popular, scoring above other infrastructure in opinion polls despite the efforts of climate denialists to portray it as a public nuisance. Most importantly, it is renewable and very low-carbon. Unlike oil, gas and coal, wind does not produce greenhouse gases and is not something we can run out of. Unlike nuclear, it does not produce toxic waste as a byproduct.

The government's climate advisers say that onshore wind power capacity will need to triple in 15 years if the UK is to meet the target of net-zero emissions by 2050. Although this is a huge challenge, the good news is that the UK's wind sector is already a world-beating one. While the solar power industry was seriously damaged by the removal of subsidies, wind companies were able to thrive.

Ministers must not be allowed to sit on their laurels. Wind and solar will not solve all our energy problems and research and development into battery storage, carbon capture and renewable power projects of all kinds are urgently needed. Systematic retrofitting of the UK's aged housing stock, to increase energy efficiency, has been shamefully neglected. Having promised that the public will, in future, have a greater say over wind developments through an altered planning process, ministers must now ensure that all new housing and construction projects are compatible with climate goals.

But if the government should expect limited credit for reversing a destructive decision that many of its own ministers supported, the significance of this announcement should not be underestimated. Under the last two prime ministers, energy policy often appeared more ideological than rational. While environmental campaigners of all stripes argued in vain on behalf of renewables, ministers consistently sided with the oil industry.

That chapter has now ended. The UK's oil industry has all but collapsed. The influence on public life of climate deniers has dramatically waned—with 2019's upsurge of climate activism among the causes. The UK has a mountain to climb to reach emissions targets, and the government's record so far is not encouraging. But the return of onshore wind is a breath of fresh air.

文章大意

第一段：政府撤销了针对陆上风电的禁令。风能是目前最廉价的清洁能源。

第二段：英国要想实现减排目标，就必须重视风能发电。

第三段：风能和太阳能无法完全解决能源问题，政府需要从多方面做出努力。

第四段：过去的能源政策很不合理，官员们都支持石油产业。

第五段：如今英国石油产业已经崩盘，气候变化否认者失势。陆上风电的归来让人为之一振。

逐段精讲

Para. 1 The government's decision to overturn an effective five-year-old ban on new onshore wind power generation is hugely welcome. Wind provides the cheapest energy, and onshore wind is even cheaper. It is also popular, scoring above other infrastructure in opinion polls despite the efforts of climate denialists to portray it as a public nuisance. Most importantly, it is renewable and very low-carbon. Unlike oil, gas and coal, wind does not produce greenhouse gases and is not something we can run out of. Unlike nuclear, it does not produce toxic waste as a byproduct.

译文 政府撤销了一项长达五年的针对陆上风力发电的有效禁令，这一决策大受欢迎。风能是最廉价的能源，其中向岸风尤为便宜。尽管气候变化否认者努力将其说成是社会公害，向岸风还是很受欢迎，它在民意调查中的分数高于其他电力基础设施。最重要的是，风能具有可再生且低碳的特性。与石油、天然气或煤炭不同，风能不产生温室气体，本身也取之不尽、用之不竭。风能也不同于核能，风能不会产生有毒废物之类的副产品。

生词点睛

overturn v. 推翻；撤销	**ban** n. 禁令
onshore adj. 陆上的；向岸的	**score** v. 得分
nuisance n. 麻烦事；妨害行为	**toxic** adj. 有毒的
byproduct n. 副产品	

重点表达

- **portray A as B** 将 A 描绘成 B

They **portray** him **as** a weak leader, but I don't think that's a fair characterization. 他们把他说成是软弱的领袖，但我认为这种描绘有失偏颇。

- **run out of** 用光；耗尽

They have **run out of** ideas. 他们已经想不出任何办法。

Para. 2 The government's climate advisers say that onshore wind power capacity will need to triple in 15 years if the UK is to meet the target of net-zero emissions by 2050. Although this is a huge challenge, the good news is that the UK's wind sector is already a world-beating one. While the solar power industry was seriously damaged by the removal of subsidies, wind companies were able to thrive.

译文 政府的气候顾问表示，英国要想在2050年时达到零净排放的目标，其陆上风电的发电量需要在15年内增至三倍。虽然这是个巨大的挑战，但好消息在于英国的风电产业已然是世界上最先进的。尽管太阳能行业由于财政补贴的取消受到了严重的打击，但风电企业仍然有繁荣发展的能力。

生词点睛

triple v. 使增至三倍	**world-beating** adj. 举世无双的

Para. 3 Ministers must not be allowed to sit on their laurels. Wind and solar will not solve all our energy problems and research and development into battery storage, carbon capture and renewable power projects of all kinds are urgently needed. Systematic retrofitting of the UK's aged housing stock, to increase energy efficiency, has been shamefully neglected. Having promised that the public will, in future, have a greater say over wind developments through an altered planning process, ministers must now ensure that all new housing and construction projects are compatible with climate goals.

译文 不能再让官员们安于现状了。风能和太阳能无法完全解决我们的能源问题，我们亟须进行蓄电池储能、碳捕捉以及各类可再生能源项目的研发。政府一直可耻地忽略了英国老旧房屋的系统性节能翻新工作。官员们曾承诺未来会通过新的规划流程让公众在风能发展方面有更多的发言权，现在他们必须确保所有新的住房与建设项目都符合气候方面的政策目标。

生词点睛

storage n. 存储	**retrofit** v. 翻新
alter v. 改变	**compatible** adj. 兼容的；和谐相处的

重点表达

❖ **sit on one's laurels** 躺在功劳簿上；满足于既得荣誉

The Chinese are not going to **sit on their laurels** after the success of launching Shenzhou V spacecraft. 在成功发射"神舟"五号载人飞船之后，中国人并没有满足于既得荣誉。

❖ **have a greater say over sth.** 在某事上有更大的话语权

Students want to **have a greater say over** curriculum setup. 学生们希望在课程设置上有更多的发言权。

Para. 4 But if the government should expect limited credit for reversing a destructive decision that many of its own ministers supported, the significance of this announcement should not be underestimated. Under the last two prime ministers, energy policy often appeared more ideological than rational. While environmental campaigners of all stripes argued in vain on behalf of renewables, ministers consistently sided with oil industry.

译文 但如果政府是想通过撤销一个有很多官员支持的毁灭性决策来重拾信誉，那我们就不能低估本次声明的重要性。在前两任首相任期内，能源政策往往遵从意识形态而非理性。各类环保活动家对各类可再生能源的支持皆为徒劳，官员们仍然雷打不动地支持石油产业。

生词点睛

destructive adj. 毁灭性的	**significance** n. 重要性
ideological adj. 意识形态的	**side** v. 支持；偏袒

重点表达

❖ **sb. of all stripes** 各类的（人）

The most convincing argument comes from the theory of evolution, which is widely accepted by

biologists of all stripes. 其中最具说服力的理由来自生物界各流派所广泛接受的进化论。

Para. 5 That chapter has now ended. The UK's oil industry has all but collapsed. The influence on public life of climate deniers has dramatically waned—with 2019's upsurge of climate activism among the causes. The UK has a mountain to climb to reach emissions targets, and the government's record so far is not encouraging. But the return of onshore wind is a breath of fresh air.

译文 眼下这已经是老黄历了。英国的石油产业目前近乎崩盘。2019年爆棚的气候激进主义矛头直指问题的根源，气候变化否认者们对公众生活的影响力大不如前。英国要想实现其减排目标还需要克服很多困难，目前为止政府的作为不甚理想。但至少陆上风电的归来让人为之一振。

生词点睛

| **chapter** n. 章节 | **upsurge** v. 猛增；急剧上升 |

重点表达

❖ all but 几乎；差不多

The concrete wall that used to divide this city has now **all but** gone. 曾经将这座城市分隔开的混凝土墙现在已几乎不复存在。

❖ be a breath of fresh air 某事物令人耳目一新、神清气爽

His idea about revitalizing the company's activities **is a breath of fresh air**. 他使公司活动恢复元气的意见令人耳目一新。

词意选选看

1. overturn ____   a. 有毒的
2. ban ____   b. 改变
3. score ____   c. 章节
4. toxic ____   d. 支持
5. triple ____   e. 得分
6. alter ____   f. 推翻

7. destructive ____
8. side ____
9. chapter ____
10. upsurge ____

g. 猛增
h. 禁令
i. 毁灭性的
j. 使增至三倍

拓展阅读

陆上风电

Onshore wind is an inexpensive source of electric power, competitive with or in many places cheaper than coal or gas plants. Onshore wind farms also have an impact on the landscape, as typically they need to be spread over more land than other power stations and need to be built in wild and rural areas, which can lead to "industrialization of the countryside" and habitat loss. Offshore wind is steadier and stronger than on land and offshore farms have less visual impact, but construction and maintenance costs are higher.

延伸思考：陆上风电相较于海上风电有哪些优势与劣势？

专题二 科技与反思

导 言

如果说环保类话题是考研阅读中的"新贵",那么科技类话题则可称得上是"名门望族"了。从考研英语诞生之日起至今,几乎每年都有至少一篇科技类的阅读文章。

近年来,随着计算机以及互联网在人们日常生活与工作中的普及和渗透,科技与社会、民生的关系变得越发紧密;科技问题就是社会、民生问题,科技领域中无法处理的矛盾会外化为社会、民生中的矛盾。仅从近三年的阅读真题来看,就有关于"自动化与就业问题""科技巨头滥用用户信息"的话题。这些话题经历了不同分析视角下的多次考查,思辨深度也在逐年增加,如果考生不具备相关的知识积累,阅读此类文章时将会异常吃力。

考研英语的阅读文章中,对科技的看法是非常辩证的,且往往带有很强的批判性,其常见的分析角度有以下几种:1. 聚焦代表先进生产力的新科技本身;2. 阐明随着新科技的出现一起到来的难以预料的负面影响;3. 探讨新科技相关的伦理道德问题(比如克隆问题);4. 反思科研工作本身的方法论和价值观。总而言之,新科技的出现在促进生产力发展的同时,也带来了新的社会形势,而新的社会形势对人们提出了适应新常态、理解新科技、推动科技进一步发展等方面的全新挑战——即"新科技、新形势、新挑战"。

基于考研英语阅读科技类话题这种"强思辨性"的特点,本专题除了一篇文章涉及当前最热门的"AI 算法与偏见"话题外,其余文章都以对已有的科研工作、科学规律的反思为主。笔者希望通过这种方式,帮各位考生打破以前关于科技"高大上""好赞顶"的印象,逐渐锻炼考研人应有的辩证性和批判性思维。

2010—2021 年相关考研英语阅读真题

英语一

2012　Text-3　科研工作的可信性证实
2013　Text-3　对人类未来的展望
2015　Text-2　数字信息搜查权
2018　Text-1　自动化与就业问题
2019　Text-3　AI 的伦理道德问题
2021　Text-4　宽带供应商垄断和网络中立性问题

英语二

2013　Text-1　自动化时代的就业法门
2014　Text-3　自动化时代的人机协作
2017　Text-2　数码产品与亲子关系
2018　Text-3　科技巨头滥用用户信息
2021　Text-3　科技巨头并购初创企业

第 1 天

There were many failures in January 2000, from the significant to the trivial. Many credit-card systems and cash points failed. Some customers received bills for 100 years' interest while others were briefly rich for the same reason.

Internationally, 15 nuclear reactors shut down; the oil pumping station in Yumurtalik failed, cutting off supplies to Istanbul; there were power cuts in Hawaii and government computers failed in many countries. A customer at a New York state video rental store had a bill for $91,250, the cost of renting the film *The General's Daughter* for 100 years.

One serious UK problem was recognised only when a health visitor in Yorkshire noticed an unusual number of babies being born with Down's syndrome. More than 150 pregnant women were given the wrong results from tests because the computer system that was used in nine hospitals calculated the women's date of birth incorrectly from January 2000; it had worked perfectly for the previous decade. The result was that women who should have been identified as being in a high-risk category were wrongly told that they did not need further testing.

The millennium bug was real and the internationally coordinated effort was a great success. Tens of thousands of failures were prevented. Some suppliers took advantage and sold unnecessary upgrades to their customers, but those of us who worked days, nights and weekends to meet the hard deadline of December 1999 are angered when ignorant people think that because we succeeded, the threat was not serious.

The Y2K problem should be seen as a warning of the danger that arises when millions of independent systems might fail because of a single event. But this lesson has not been learned. Today, millions of systems rely on the GPS signal to provide the accurate timing, positioning and navigation on which our communications, defence, financial systems and food supplies depend. Yet the GPS signal is easy to jam and could be disabled for days or weeks by a major solar storm. Today, so many computer systems use the same software that a single cyberattack could spread rapidly and cause chaos. And 20 years ago, we did not have automated just-in-time supply chains with their much greater vulnerability.

Twenty years ago we showed that committed international action could overcome a critical threat. We shall need that commitment again.

文章大意

第一至三段：2000年，千年虫问题在国际上和英国国内造成了大大小小的各类问题。

第四段：千年虫危机在国际社会的共同努力下最终得以及时解决，但这也导致很多人没有意识到此次危机的严重性。

第五段：千年虫问题的本质是大规模的系统性失灵，这一教训并未被吸取。当今的 GPS 系统和标准化的电脑系统仍可能发生类似的问题。

第六段：类似千年虫的问题可能即将再度发生，到时仍需国际社会协力度过危机。

逐段精讲

Para. 1 There were many failures in January 2000, from the significant to the trivial. Many credit-card systems and cash points failed. Some customers received bills for 100 years' interest while others were briefly rich for the same reason.

译文 2000年1月发生了大大小小的诸多事故与问题。很多信用卡系统以及取款机失灵。有些顾客收到了收取100年利息费用的账单，也有人因为相同的原因暴富。

生词点睛

failure *n.* 事故；失败	trivial *adj.* 琐碎的；不值一提的
bill *n.* 账单；法案	interest *n.* 利息；利益；兴趣

重点表达

❖ from the *adj.* to the *adj.* 从某类事物到某类事物

The disaster affects everyone equally, **from the affluent to the poor**. 这场灾难波及了所有人，不论贫富。

Para. 2 Internationally, 15 nuclear reactors shut down; the oil pumping station in Yumurtalik failed, cutting off supplies to Istanbul; there were power cuts in Hawaii and government computers failed in many countries. A customer at a New York state video rental store had a bill for $91,250, the cost of renting the film *The General's Daughter* for 100 years.

译文 全球范围内，15个核反应堆关停；尤穆尔塔勒克的采油泵站停转，因而切断了对伊斯坦布尔的石油供应；夏威夷发生了断电，很多国家的政府机关电脑失灵。纽约州一位音像出租店的顾客收到了高达91 250美元的账单，这笔费用足以租赁《将军的女儿》这部电影的录像带100年。

生词点睛

nuclear reactor 核反应堆	pump v. 用泵排出
power cut 断电	rental adj. 租赁的

重点表达

❖ shut down sth. 关停

The company was **shut down**, and its business licenses (was) revoked. 公司被关停，公司的营业执照也被吊销了。

Para. 3 One serious UK problem was recognised only when a health visitor in Yorkshire noticed an unusual number of babies being born with Down's syndrome. More than 150 pregnant women were given the wrong results from tests because the computer system that was used in nine hospitals calculated the women's date of birth incorrectly from January 2000; it had worked perfectly for the previous decade. The result was that women who should have been identified as being in a high-risk category were wrongly told that they did not need further testing.

译文 英国也发生了一个严重的事故，当时约克郡一位保健员发现患唐氏综合征的新生儿数量不正常，人们这才意识到出了问题。当地九家医院使用的计算机系统在过去十年里运行得极其正常，但这次错误地将孕妇的出生日期算成了2000年1月，超过150名孕妇因此拿到了错误的诊断结果。这导致那些本该被划为高危人群的孕妇收到了并不需要进一步诊断的错误通知。

生词点睛

syndrome *n.* 综合征；症状	**pregnant** *adj.* 怀孕的
calculate *v.* 计算	**previous** *adj.* 先前的

重点表达

❖ **be identified as** 被认为是；被认定是

China **is identified as** central to almost every global issue in the coming year, from the economy to climate change and nuclear diplomacy. 未来，中国将在经济发展、气候变化到核外交斡旋等几乎所有全球事务中处于中心地位。

❖ **in the high-risk category**（是）高危人群

High blood pressure, smoking, obesity, diabetes or a strong family history of the disease can put someone **in the high-risk category** of heart attack. 患有高血压、肥胖症、糖尿病以及吸烟或者有严重家族病史的人，都是患心脏疾病的高危人群。

Para. 4 The millennium bug was real and the internationally coordinated effort was a great success. Tens of thousands of failures were prevented. Some suppliers took advantage and sold unnecessary upgrades to their customers, but those of us who worked days, nights and weekends to meet the hard deadline of December 1999 are angered when ignorant people think that because we succeeded, the threat was not serious.

译文 千年虫是个真实存在的漏洞，而当时国际上的协同努力则是一次重大的成功，成千上万的问题因此被阻止。部分软件供应商借着千年虫危机发了财，他们向顾客兜售非必要的升级服务；我们中那些为了赶在1999年12月的最后期限前解决问题而日以继夜、奋战数周的人却被激怒了，因为一些不明真相的人认为，我们的胜利说明这次危机本身没什么大不了的。

生词点睛

millennium *n.* 千禧年	**coordinated** *adj.* 协作的
upgrade *n.* 升级	**ignorant** *adj.* 无辜的

重点表达

❖ **take advantage of sth.** 利用；占便宜

It takes some brains to seize these opportunities and to **take advantage of** them. 需要绞尽脑汁才能发现掩藏的机遇并且利用好它们。

❖ **meet the deadline** 赶上最后期限

The boss called him to account for failing to **meet the deadline**. 老板让他解释未能按时完成任务的原因。

Para. 5 **The Y2K problem** should be seen as a warning of the danger that arises when millions of independent systems might fail because of a single event. But this lesson has not been learned. Today, millions of systems rely on the GPS signal to provide the accurate timing, positioning and navigation on which our communications, defence, financial systems and food supplies depend. Yet the GPS signal is easy to jam and could be disabled for days or weeks by a major solar storm. Today, so many computer systems use the same software that a single cyberattack could spread rapidly and cause chaos. And 20 years ago, we did not have automated just-in-time supply chains with their much greater vulnerability.

译文 千年虫问题应该被当作一次危险警示，上百万个相互独立的系统可能会因为某个事件而陷入集体瘫痪。但人们并未吸取这一教训。时至今日，数百万系统都依赖 GPS 信号来提供准确的计时、定位以及导航，GPS 信号支撑着我们的通信、国防、金融系统以及食物供给。但 GPS 信号很容易中断，一次大型的太阳风暴就可以使之失灵数天甚至数周。如今，太多的计算机系统都使用相同的软件，以至于单次网络攻击可以快速传播并引发混乱。20 年前，我们没有自动化的实时供应链，也更易受到此类问题的影响。

背景知识

the Y2K problem：计算机 2000 年问题，又叫作"千年虫问题"，缩写为"Y2K"。是指在某些使用了计算机程序的智能系统中，由于其中的年份只使用两位十进制数来表示，因此当系统进行跨世纪的日期处理运算时，就会出现错误的结果，进而引发各种各样的系统功能紊乱甚至崩溃。

生词点睛

arise *v.* 出现；上升	**accurate** *adj.* 准确的
timing *n.* 计时；对时机的把握	**navigation** *n.* 导航
jam *v.* 卡壳；无法运转	**disable** *v.* 使无效
solar storm 太阳风暴	**cyberattack** *n.* 网络攻击
automated *adj.* 自动化的	**just-in-time** *adj.* 实时的

重点表达

❖ (sth.) arise （某种问题）出现、浮现

You have to take action and deal with problems as they **arise**. 你必须在问题出现的时候及时采取行动进行处理。

❖ rely on sth. to do sth. 依赖某物来做某事

We should cultivate habits for exercising skepticism about what we read, because we cannot **rely on** the journal editors or the media and bloggers **to** be skeptical for us. 我们应该培养对所读内容进行质疑的习惯，因为我们不能依靠期刊编辑或是媒体博主来替我们质疑。

Para. 6 Twenty years ago we showed that committed international action could overcome a critical threat. We shall need that commitment again.

译文 二十年前我们通过行动证明，国际社会齐心协力就可以战胜重大危机。如今我们可能需要再次携手行动。

生词点睛

committed *adj.* 尽心尽力的	**critical threat** 重大危机

• 词意选选看 •

1. trivial ____
2. bill ____

a. 无辜的
b. 自动化的

3. interest ____
4. rental ____
5. pregnant ____
6. millennium ____
7. ignorant ____
8. arise ____
9. navigation ____
10. automated ____

c. 账单
d. 琐碎的
e. 出现
f. 导航
g. 租赁的
h. 怀孕的
i. 千禧年
j. 利益

·拓展阅读·

以史为鉴

1. The history holds the key to the future.
   历史是通往未来的钥匙。

2. The only thing we learn from history is that we learn nothing from history. —Hegel
   我们从历史中学到的唯一教训就是我们从未学到任何教训。——黑格尔

延伸思考： 结合以上内容，思考以史为鉴的必要性及困难性所在。

第 2 天

One of the things that really annoys AI researchers is how supposedly "intelligent" machines are judged by much higher standards than are humans. Take self-driving cars, they say. So far they've driven millions of miles with very few accidents, a tiny number of them fatal. Yet whenever an autonomous vehicle kills someone there's a huge hoo-ha, while every year in the US nearly 40,000 people die in crashes involving conventional vehicles.

Likewise, the AI enthusiasts complain, everybody and his dog (this columnist included) is up in arms about algorithmic bias: the way in which automated decision-making systems embody the racial, gender and other prejudices implicit in the data sets on which they were trained. And yet society is apparently content to endure the astonishing irrationality of much human decision-making.

In judging the debate about whether human intelligence (HI) is always superior to the artificial intelligence (AI), are we humans just demonstrating how irrational we can be? Yes, says Jason Collins, a behavioural and data scientist who now works for PwC Australia. In a satirical article in the online journal *Behavioral Scientist*, he turns the question we routinely ask about AI on its head: "Before humans become the standard way in which we make decisions," he writes, "we need to consider the risks and ensure implementation of human decision-making systems does not cause widespread harm."

This is a good source of belly laughs for AI enthusiasts, but actually there's a serious edge to it. For example, although bias is intrinsic in all machine-learning systems—and is just as common as it is in human decision-making systems—nevertheless, biased algorithms may be easier to fix than biased people.

That, at any rate, is the conclusion of a couple of empirical studies of racial bias in recruitment and healthcare published in the *American Economic Review and Science*. It turned out that uncovering algorithmic bias was relatively easy—it's basically a statistical exercise. "The work was technical and rote, requiring neither stealth nor resourcefulness," a researcher wrote. The humans in the system, on the other hand, were a different story. The researchers found them "mysterious", and discovered that "changing people's hearts and minds is no simple matter". Changing biased algorithms was easier than changing people: "software on computers can be updated; the 'wetware' in our brains has so far proven much less pliable".

文章大意

第一段：人们习惯于以更严苛的标准去要求 AI，这可以从自动驾驶汽车造成伤亡时社会的反应中看出来。

第二、三段：我们对算法中的各种偏见大加反对，却对人类本身决策时的非理性行为无动于衷；更容易犯错误的人类可能没有资格去评价 AI 的决策水平。

第四、五段：人类对 AI 如此严苛的原因可能在于，有偏见的算法比有偏见的人更容易纠正。最新的论文也论证了这一点，AI 算法可以升级，但人心远没有这样的可塑性。

逐段精讲

Para. 1 One of the things that really annoys AI researchers is how supposedly "intelligent" machines are judged by much higher standards than are humans. Take self-driving cars, they say. So far they've driven millions of miles with very few accidents, a tiny number of them fatal. Yet whenever an autonomous vehicle kills someone there's a huge hoo-ha, while every year in the US nearly 40,000 people die in crashes involving conventional vehicles.

译文 相比于对人类的评判，人们采取高得多的标准来审判据称"智能"的机器，这让 AI 科研人员甚是气恼。以自动驾驶汽车为例，截至目前它们已经行驶了上百万公里，造成的事故寥寥无几，致人死亡的情况更是屈指可数。但每当自动驾驶汽车致人死亡时，总是引起一片哗然；而美国每年有近四万人死于与传统汽车有关的车祸。

生词点睛

supposedly *adv.* 据说；据传	**fatal** *adj.* 致命的
autonomous vehicle 自动驾驶汽车	**crash** *n.* 碰撞；撞车

重点表达

❖ **involve sth.** 涉及；牵连；需要某事物

Managing an army **involves** lots of discipline. 管理军队需要讲究纪律。

I find myself **involved** in a dangerous situation. 我发现自己被卷入了危险之中。

Para. 2 Likewise, the AI enthusiasts complain, everybody and his dog (this columnist included) is up in arms about algorithmic bias: the way in which automated decision-making systems embody the racial, gender and other prejudices implicit in the data sets on which they were trained. And yet society is apparently content to endure the astonishing irrationality of much human decision-making.

译文 同样，AI 的支持者们还抱怨称，每个人（包括笔者在内）都强烈反对算法中的偏见：自动决策系统如何体现出 AI 接受训练时所使用的数据集中的种族、性别或其他偏见。但我们的社会显然能接受人类在决策过程中表现出的那种令人震惊的不理性行为。

生词点睛

columnist n. 专栏作家	algorithmic adj. 算法的
embody v. 体现；包含	irrationality n. 非理性；不理性

重点表达

❖ **be up in arms about sth.** 强烈抗议某事；对某事非常不满

Residents **are up in arms about** the closure of the local library. 居民对当地图书馆的关闭非常不满。

❖ **implicit in sth.** 内含于某事物中的

You should learn from the lessons **implicit in** the failure of your marriage. 你要从婚姻的失败中吸取教训。

Para. 3 In judging the debate about whether human intelligence (HI) is always superior to the artificial intelligence (AI), are we humans just demonstrating how irrational we can be? Yes, says Jason Collins, a behavioural and data scientist who now works for **PwC** Australia. In a satirical article in the online journal *Behavioral Scientist*, he turns the question we routinely ask about AI on its head: "Before humans become the standard way in which we make decisions," he writes, "we need to consider the risks and ensure implementation of human decision-making systems does not cause widespread harm."

译文 在关于人类智慧是否总是高于人工智能的争论中，人类不是刚好体现出了自己的非理性程度吗？现任职于澳大利亚普华永道的行为与数据科学家杰森·柯林斯对此表示认同。在互联网期刊《行为科学家》的一篇讽刺性文章中，他将我们日常对 AI 提出的问题指向了人类自身，柯林斯写道："在人类成为标准的决策方式前，我们应该考虑其中的风险，并确保采用人类决策系统不会造成广泛的危害。"

背景知识

PwC：普华永道会计师事务所（PricewaterhouseCoopers）是国际四大会计师事务所之一，与其并列的其他三大所分别是毕马威、德勤和安永。

生词点睛

artificial *adj.* 人工的；非自然的	**satirical** *adj.* 讽刺的
journal *n.* 期刊；杂志	**implementation** *n.* 应用；落实；实施

重点表达

❖ be superior to sth. 优于某事物

I've personally never subscribed to the view that either sex **is superior to** the other. 我个人从来都不认为性别有优劣之分。

❖ turn sth. on its head 颠覆某观点；以全新视角审视某事

Anytime something annoying and frustrating occurs, **turn it on its head** and find the humor. 如果有令人苦恼或沮丧的事情发生，请换个角度找找它幽默的地方。

Para. 4 This is a good source of belly laughs for AI enthusiasts, but actually there's a serious edge to it. For example, although bias is intrinsic in all machine-learning systems—and is just as common as it is in human decision-making systems—nevertheless, biased algorithms may be easier to fix than biased people.

译文 虽然这对AI爱好者们来说是个很好的笑料，但其中也有值得深思的地方。正如人类决策系统中普遍存在偏见一样，虽然偏见也存在于所有的机器学习系统中，但有偏见的算法可能比有偏见的人更容易纠正。

生词点睛

belly laugh 捧腹大笑	**edge** *n.* 边缘
intrinsic *adj.* 固有的；内在的	**nevertheless** *adv.* 但是；然而

Para. 5 That, at any rate, is the conclusion of a couple of empirical studies of racial bias in recruitment and healthcare published in the *American Economic Review and Science*. It turned out that uncovering algorithmic bias was relatively easy—it's basically a statistical exercise. "The work was technical and rote, requiring neither stealth nor resourcefulness," a researcher wrote. The humans in the system, on the other hand, were a different story. The researchers found them "mysterious", and discovered that "changing people's hearts and minds is no simple matter". Changing biased algorithms was easier than changing people: "software on computers can be updated; the 'wetware' in our brains has so far proven much less pliable".

译文 无论如何，这正是《美国经济评论与科学》杂志上发表的几个实证研究报告的结论，这些实证研究主要关于招聘与医疗领域的种族偏见问题。事实上，发现算法中的偏见其实是相对容易的，其本质是一种统计行为。一位研究人员写道："这是项技术性且机械性的工作，既不需要明察暗访，也不需要多大的智慧。"而涉及人的问题，情况就完全不一样了。研究人员认为人类"难以捉摸"，他们发现"改变人心并非易事"。改变带有偏见的算法比改变人更容易："电脑中的软件可以升级；但我们脑中的'湿件'展现出的可塑性则差得多。"

专题二 科技与反思

生词点睛

empirical *adj.* 经验性的；实证的	**exercise** *n.* 行为；做法；实践
rote *n.* 死记硬背	**stealth** *n.* 潜行；偷偷摸摸
resourcefulness *n.* 足智多谋	**pliable** *adj.* 可塑的；易受影响的

重点表达

❖ it turns out that... 真相是……；结果是……

It turns out that this therapy does not work well. 事实证明这个疗法效果不佳。

❖ be a different story（表转折）某事上，情况则完全不同了

Learning English is easy, but French **is a different story**. 学英语很简单，但学法语可就是另一回事了。

词意选选看

1. supposedly ____
2. crash ____
3. algorithm ____
4. irrationality ____
5. artificial ____
6. implementation ____
7. nevertheless ____
8. empirical ____
9. exercise ____
10. pliable ____

a. 人工的
b. 据说
c. 经验的
d. 实施
e. 然而
f. 可塑的
g. 算法
h. 撞车
i. 非理性
j. 做法

拓展阅读

回音壁效应

  In social life, echo chamber is a metaphorical description of a situation in which beliefs are amplified or reinforced by communication and repetition inside a closed system. By visiting an "echo chamber", people are able to seek out information that reinforces their existing views, potentially as an unconscious exercise of confirmation bias. This may increase social and political polarization and extremism.

延伸思考：算法偏见与回音壁效应有哪些内在联系？

第 3 天

Way back in the 1960s, Gordon Moore, the co-founder of Intel, observed that the number of transistors that could be fitted on a silicon chip was doubling every two years. Since the transistor count is related to processing power, that meant that computing power was effectively doubling every two years. Thus was born Moore's law, which for most people working in the computer industry—or at any rate those younger than 40—has provided the kind of bedrock certainty that Newton's laws of motion did for mechanical engineers.

But computing involves a combination of hardware and software and one of the predictable consequences of Moore's law is that it made programmers lazier. Writing software is a craft and some people are better at it than others. They write code that is more elegant and, more importantly, leaner, so that it executes faster. In the early days, when the hardware was relatively primitive, craftsmanship really mattered. When Bill Gates was a lad, for example, he wrote a Basic interpreter for one of the earliest microcomputers, the TRS-80. Because the machine had only a tiny read-only memory, Gates had to fit it into just 16 kilobytes. He wrote it in assembly language to increase efficiency and save space; there's a legend that for years afterwards he could recite the entire program by heart.

There are thousands of stories like this from the early days of computing. But as Moore's law took hold, the need to write lean code gradually disappeared and incentives changed. Programming became industrialised as "software engineering". The construction of sprawling software ecosystems such as operating systems and commercial applications required large teams of developers; these then caused associated bureaucracies of project managers and executives. Large software projects morphed into the kind of death march memorably chronicled in Fred Brooks's celebrated book, *The Mythical Man-Month*, which was published in 1975 and has never been out of print, for the very good reason that it's still relevant. And in the process, software became bloated and often inefficient.

But this didn't matter because the hardware was always delivering the computing power that concealed the "bloatware" problem. As Moore's law reaches the end of its dominion, we basically have only two options: either we moderate our ambitions or we go back to writing leaner, more efficient code. In other words, back to the future.

文章大意

第一段：摩尔定律表明，硬件运算能力每两年就会提高一倍。

第二段：硬件运算能力的快速提高会导致程序员变懒。过去硬件落后时，程序员会努力写出更加简练高效的代码。

第三段：随着硬件的发展以及对复杂软件系统的需求，开发者不再追求代码的简练高效，官僚主义现象进一步导致如今代码的臃肿低效。

第四段：硬件运算能力快速提高的阶段即将结束，我们应该重新以简练高效的代码为目标。

逐段精讲

Para. 1 Way back in the 1960s, Gordon Moore, the co-founder of Intel, observed that the number of transistors that could be fitted on a silicon chip was doubling every two years. Since the transistor count is related to processing power, that meant that computing power was effectively doubling every two years. Thus was born Moore's law, which for most people working in the computer industry—or at any rate those younger than 40—has provided the kind of bedrock certainty that Newton's laws of motion did for mechanical engineers.

译文 早在20世纪60年代，英特尔公司的联合创始人戈登·摩尔就发现，一个硅芯片上可以容纳的晶体管数量每两年会翻一番。由于晶体管数量的多少与处理能力相关，上述情况就意味着运算能力每两年会提高一倍。摩尔定律便由此诞生了；对于大部分计算机从业人员，或至少是对于其中40岁以下的人而言，摩尔定律的可靠性就好比机械工程领域中的牛顿运动定律。

生词点睛

transistor n. 晶体管	**bedrock** n. 基石
certainty n. 确定性	**motion** n. 运动

重点表达

❖ **thus was born sth.** 某事物便由此诞生了

Thus was born the quantity theory of money, which has survived to this day. 货币数量理论便由此诞生，并一直沿用至今。

Para. 2 But computing involves a combination of hardware and software and one of the predictable consequences of Moore's law is that it made programmers lazier. Writing software is a craft and some people are better at it than others. They write code that is more elegant and, more importantly, leaner, so that it executes faster. In the early days, when the hardware was relatively primitive, craftsmanship really mattered. When Bill Gates was a lad, for example, he wrote a Basic interpreter for one of the earliest microcomputers, the TRS-80. Because the machine had only a tiny read-only memory, Gates had to fit it into just 16 kilobytes. He wrote it in assembly language to increase efficiency and save space; there's a legend that for years afterwards he could recite the entire program by heart.

译文　然而计算需要硬件与软件相结合，摩尔定律带来的其中一个可以预见的后果是，它使程序员们变得更懒惰了。编写软件是一门技艺，有些人就是比其他人更擅长此事。他们写的代码更简练，更重要的是，这些代码更加高效，所以执行起来就更快。在早年硬件还相对落后的时期，技艺尤为重要。举例来说，当比尔·盖茨还是个小伙子的时候，他给最早的微型电脑之———TRS-80 写过一个 Basic 解释程序。由于这部机器只有很小的只读内存，所以盖茨不得不把这个软件的体积控制在 16kb 以内。为了让程序更高效并节省空间，他用汇编语言进行了编写；有传言说多年之后他仍然可以背出该程序的全部代码。

生词点睛

combination n. 组合	**predictable** adj. 可预见的
craft n. 手艺；技艺	**lean** adj. 高效的；瘦的
execute v. 执行	**primitive** adj. 落后的；原始的
craftsmanship n. 手艺；精工细作	**lad** n. 小伙子
kilobyte n. 千字节	**legend** n. 传奇

重点表达

❖ **fit into** 刚好放入；融入（某种情形）

The car was too big to **fit into** our garage. 这部车太大了，我们的车库放不下。

I don't think she'll **fit into** the organization. 我认为她不适合参加这个组织。

Para. 3 There are thousands of stories like this from the early days of computing. But as Moore's law took hold, the need to write lean code gradually disappeared and incentives changed. Programming became industrialised as "software engineering". The construction of sprawling software ecosystems such as operating systems and commercial applications required large teams of developers; these then caused associated bureaucracies of project managers and executives. Large software projects morphed into the kind of death march memorably chronicled in Fred Brooks's celebrated book, *The Mythical Man-Month*, which was published in 1975 and has never been out of print, for the very good reason that it's still relevant. And in the process, software became bloated and often inefficient.

译文 在计算机时代早期，像这样的故事还有很多。但随着摩尔定律主导了计算机的发展，编写简练代码的需求逐渐消失了，程序员们的激励机制也发生了变化。编程工作变成了产业化的"软件工程"。诸如操作系统和商业应用等杂乱无章的软件生态系统的建设需要大量的开发者队伍；由此形成了项目经理与高管组成的官僚体系。大型软件开发项目变成了死亡之旅，弗雷德里克·布鲁克斯在他的名作《人月神话》中对此类情况做了生动的记录，该书自1975年出版以来从未停印，因为其内容时至今日仍然有指导意义。在这一过程中，软件变得臃肿且往往低效。

背景知识

The Mythical Man-Month：《人月神话》，作者是"图灵奖"获得者弗雷德里克·布鲁克斯，该书内容源于作者在IBM公司任软件系统项目经理时的实践经验。

生词点睛

sprawling *adj.* 杂乱蔓延的	**developer** *n.* （软件）开发者
bureaucracy *n.* 官僚作风	**morph** *v.* 变形
chronicle *v.* （按发生顺序）记载	**bloated** *adj.* 膨胀的

重点表达

❖ **take hold** 占主导地位

She was determined not to let the illness **take hold** again. 她决心再也不让疾病击垮自己。

❖ **morph into** 变形为；转变为

It was like watching him **morph into** an adult right before my eyes. 这感觉就像是我眼瞅着他在我面前变成大人。

Para. 4 But this didn't matter because the hardware was always delivering the computing power that concealed the "bloatware" problem. As Moore's law reaches the end of its dominion, we basically have only two options: either we moderate our ambitions or we go back to writing leaner, more efficient code. In other words, back to the future.

译文 但这在以前没什么影响，因为硬件方面带来的计算能力的提升总会掩盖"膨胀件"的问题。如今摩尔定律的支配地位即将结束，我们基本只有两种选择：要么降低目标，要么像以前那样去写更简练高效的代码。换言之，回到未来。

生词点睛

dominion *n.* 统治（权）；支配	**option** *n.* 选择
moderate *v.* 缓和；使适中	

词意选选看

1. certainty ____   a. 执行
2. motion ____   b. 传奇
3. combination ____   c. 确定性
4. craft ____   d. 官僚作风
5. lean ____   e. 缓和
6. execute ____   f. 技艺
7. legend ____   g. 运动
8. bureaucracy ____   h. 选择

9. option ____
10. moderate ____

i. 高效的
j. 组合

拓展阅读

摩尔定律的负面影响

　　A negative implication of Moore's law is obsolescence, that is, as technologies continue to rapidly "improve", these improvements may be significant enough to render predecessor technologies obsolete rapidly. In situations in which security and survivability of hardware or data are paramount, or in which resources are limited, rapid obsolescence may pose obstacles to smooth or continued operations. Because of the toxic materials used in the production of modern computers, obsolescence, if not properly managed, may lead to harmful environmental impacts.

延伸思考：科技的快速进步可能会带来哪些方面的负面影响？

第 4 天

Albert Einstein once remarked that God is subtle, but not malicious. The material world, he thought, was unpredictable. This made the world interesting but not impenetrable. Seen like this, science advances as much through what thinkers get right as what they get wrong. A scientific theory aims to understand the world. But it is only when nature reveals an error that it can be refined.

Progress always involves making mistakes and then recognising them. That is because we are all struggling to understand why and how things are the way they are. When Dyson, an insightful and brilliant theoretical physicist, considered the idea that the limit to an energy supply that a species could have is all of the starlight in their solar system, logic would dictate that a sophisticated civilisation would build a structure to harness the entire power of its sun. This seemed eccentric at the time. Yet in 2015 it was discovered that a star 1,500 light years away was being shielded by matter circling the star. The speculation was that this mass could be the "Dyson Sphere".

A scientist will be kindly judged if led astray by a false hypothesis. Their reputation, however, may not survive if the work is sloppy or if they claim to have discovered a fact that turns out to be wrong. There is a concern, especially in social sciences and medicine, about the prevalence of studies that have proved impossible to reproduce. If the original errors do not get corrected when scientists try to take the work further, then science's capacity to remedy itself will be called into question. There are questions here about the value system in academic publishing and the funding mechanisms that have led to too many researchers thinking it is fine to move on from mistakes without publicly acknowledging them.

Science must be self-correcting and allow for even its greatest practitioners to be wrong. History is littered with examples of major figures who erred. Charles Darwin is famous for his theory of evolution by natural selection but came up with a bizarre—and mistaken—theory to explain why inheritance is a random process. It was Gregor Mendel, the father of genetics, who worked out the first set of rules of heredity. Mendel's brilliance was unrecognised in his lifetime and he finally left science for God, later becoming an abbot. In every century and every science there are brilliant blunders. The trick is to learn from them.

文章大意

第一段：正确与错误对于科研工作来说同样重要。

第二段：进步的过程总伴随着犯错与纠错，"戴森球"设想就是个很好的例子。

第三段：当前大量无法复现的研究与学术激励的机制问题，使得科学界丧失了必要的纠错能力。

第四段：科学界既要允许科研工作者犯错，也要具有纠错能力。从错误中吸取教训才是进步的关键。

逐段精讲

Para. 1 Albert Einstein once remarked that God is subtle, but not malicious. The material world, he thought, was unpredictable. This made the world interesting but not impenetrable. Seen like this, science advances as much through what thinkers get right as what they get wrong. A scientific theory aims to understand the world. But it is only when nature reveals an error that it can be refined.

译文 阿尔伯特·爱因斯坦曾说过，上帝虽然不可捉摸，但并无恶意。他认为物质世界是无法预测的，这让世界变得有趣但并非无法理解。如此看来，科学的进步一半要归功于科学家的正确，另一半则归功于他们的错误。科学理论旨在理解这个世界。但只有当大自然揭示其错误时，科学理论才能得以改进。

生词点睛

subtle *adj.* 微妙的；机智的；狡猾的	**malicious** *adj.* 恶毒的
impenetrable *adj.* 难以理解的；不可穿透的	**reveal** *v.* 揭示；显示

Para. 2 Progress always involves making mistakes and then recognising them. That is because

译文 进步的过程总伴随着犯错与纠正。这是因为我们都在竭力理解事

we are all struggling to understand why and how things are the way they are. When Dyson, an insightful and brilliant theoretical physicist, considered the idea that the limit to an energy supply that a species could have is all of the starlight in their solar system, logic would dictate that a sophisticated civilisation would build a structure to harness the entire power of its sun. This seemed eccentric at the time. Yet in 2015 it was discovered that a star 1,500 light years away was being shielded by matter circling the star. The speculation was that this mass could be the "Dyson Sphere".

物的本质及其发展规律。戴森是个极具洞察力与智慧的理论物理学家,当他想到一个物种所能得到的全部能量供给的上限就是其所处太阳系中所有光能的总和时,逻辑告诉他,一个高度发达的文明会建造一个能利用其太阳全部能量的结构体。这个想法在当时听上去很怪异。然而2015年人们发现,1 500光年外的一个星球正被某种物质环绕遮盖着。有人猜测,这可能正是"戴森球"。

生词点睛

insightful *adj.* 富有洞察力的	**theoretical** *adj.* 理论的
dictate *v.* (逻辑或常识)使人相信;口述	**harness** *v.* 控制;利用
eccentric *adj.* 奇怪的	**shield** *v.* 遮挡;庇护

重点表达

❖ **struggle to do sth.** 挣扎、努力做某事

We are determined to **struggle to** transform the mountain area in five years. 大家决心苦战五年,改变山区的面貌。

Para. 3 A scientist will be kindly judged if led astray by a false hypothesis. Their reputation, however, may not survive if the work is sloppy or if they claim to have discovered a fact that turns out to be wrong. There is a concern, especially in social sciences and medicine, about the prevalence of studies

译文 被错误的假设所误导的科学家会受到从宽对待。但如果他们工作马虎草率,抑或声称发现了某个事实但后来被证明有误的话,他们的名声可能就不保了。大量无法复现的科学研究的存在让人担忧,尤其是在社科

that have proved impossible to reproduce. If the original errors do not get corrected when scientists try to take the work further, then science's capacity to remedy itself will be called into question. There are questions here about the value system in academic publishing and the funding mechanisms that have led to too many researchers thinking it is fine to move on from mistakes without publicly acknowledging them.

和医学领域。如果科学家们做进一步研究时没能够纠正那些根源上的错误，那么科学界自我纠错的能力就不再可靠了。这也涉及学术出版和出资机制中的价值评估系统存在的问题，当前机制使得太多的科研人员觉得在不公开承认错误的情况下继续研究是可以接受的做法。

生词点睛

hypothesis *n.* 假说	**sloppy** *adj.* 马虎的；草率的
reproduce *v.* 复现	**remedy** *v.* 改进；纠正
mechanism *n.* 机制	**publicly** *adv.* 公开地

重点表达

❖ be led astray 被引入歧途

The judge thought he'd **been led astray** by older children. 法官认为他被那些年长的孩子们误导了。

❖ be called into question 受到质疑

This time the world financial system is supposedly going to collapse and capitalism is **being called into question**. 这次全球金融体系被认为行将崩溃，资本主义也正受到质疑。

Para. 4 Science must be self-correcting and allow for even its greatest practitioners to be wrong. History is littered with examples of major figures who erred. Charles Darwin is famous for his theory of evolution by natural selection but came up with a bizarre—and mistaken—theory to explain why inheritance is a random process. It was Gregor

译文 科学一定要具有自我纠错的能力，并且能够允许哪怕是最伟大的科学家犯错。大人物犯错的例子在历史上比比皆是。查尔斯·达尔文因其自然选择进化论而闻名于世，但他为解释遗传过程的随机性而提出了一个古怪且错误的理论。提出第一组遗传

Mendel, the father of genetics, who worked out the first set of rules of heredity. Mendel's brilliance was unrecognised in his lifetime and he finally left science for God, later becoming an abbot. In every century and every science there are brilliant blunders. The trick is to learn from them.

学定律的是遗传学之父——格雷戈尔·孟德尔。生前才华不为世人所知的他，最后把科学工作留给了上帝，后来去做了修道院院长。任何时代、任何科研领域中都有聪明人犯下种种愚蠢的错误，关键是要从错误中汲取教训。

生词点睛

practitioner *n.* 从业人员	**figure** *n.* 人物；数字；身形
err *v.* 犯错	**bizarre** *adj.* 奇怪的
inheritance *n.* 遗传	**heredity** *n.* 遗传
abbot *n.* 修道院院长	**blunder** *n.* 愚蠢的错误

重点表达

❖ be littered with 充斥着，充满了

Charles' speech **is littered with** lots of marketing buzzwords like "package" and "product". 查尔斯的演讲充斥着"包装""产品"之类的营销领域流行用语。

词意选选看

1. subtle ____
2. reveal ____
3. insightful ____
4. dictate ____
5. harness ____
6. eccentric ____
7. shield ____
8. hypothesis ____
9. mechanism ____

a. 富有洞察力的
b. 假说
c. 奇怪的
d. 利用
e. 纠正
f. 微妙的
g. 机制
h. 使人相信
i. 揭示

10. remedy ____   j. 遮挡

• 拓展阅读 •

戴森球

　　A Dyson sphere is a hypothetical megastructure that completely encompasses a star and captures a large percentage of its power output. The concept is a thought experiment that attempts to explain how a spacefaring civilization would meet its energy requirements once those requirements exceed what can be generated from the home planet's resources alone. Only a tiny fraction of a star's energy emissions reach the surface of any orbiting planet. Building structures encircling a star would enable a civilization to harvest far more energy.

延伸思考：戴森球概念的背后是一种怎样的思考问题的方式？

第 5 天

Underrepresentation of nonwhite ethnic groups in scientific research and clinical trials has been a disturbing trend. One particularly troubling aspect is that human genomic databases are heavily skewed toward people of European descent. If left unaddressed, this inherent bias will continue to contribute to uneven success rates in so-called precision medicine.

The problem stems from the underlying structure of science. In the early days of genomics, funding for sequencing projects was often highest among mostly white countries, so those populations are better represented in public databases. Also, some minorities have been historically mistreated by scientists—the Tuskegee syphilis experiment is one glaring example—and many members of those groups can be understandably reluctant to enter studies.

Early studies were also biased by the types of genetic variation the research focused on. Initially scientists looked at only tiny, single-base-pair DNA differences between populations, ignoring larger variations that were more difficult to assess but that turned out to be more significant than anyone expected. These are now known to cause genetic disease and influence the way drugs are metabolized by different ethnic populations, not just individuals—and advanced technologies allow scientists to identify variations that in many cases have never been seen before.

This is an exciting step forward: we are finding that some of these structural differences can explain diseases for which no cause had previously been found—such as Carney complex, a rare disorder that causes tumors to appear in various parts of the body, for example, or a mutation that may contribute to bipolar disorder and schizophrenia. And here, too, the effects may well vary from one ethnic group to another.

In the field of rare diseases, genome sequencing has proved remarkable at increasing the diagnosis rate, giving answers to patients who might otherwise have gone undiagnosed. Today that approach remains most effective for Caucasian patients because more of their DNA can be interpreted using current genomic data repositories. But as we build up data for people of other ethnicities, we can expect such successes to extend rapidly to patients of any background, which stands to dramatically improve health care for hundreds of millions of people.

Achieving the vision of precision medicine for individuals of any ethnic group requires more diverse representation in the biological repositories that underlie clinical programs. Advanced

DNA-sequencing technology is one tool of many needed to help generate better information about people from all ethnicities for the equitable application of those data in clinical practice.

文章大意

第一段：在科学研究和临床试验中，非白人种族的代表性不足。
第二段：问题源于科学的基本结构。
第三段：早期研究关注的基因变异类型存在偏见。
第四段：介绍了基因测序结构上的差异带来的益处。
第五段：在罕见疾病领域，基因组测序在提高诊断率方面具有显著的效果。
第六段：实现精准医疗的愿景需要多样化的基因数据。

逐段精讲

Para. 1 Underrepresentation of nonwhite ethnic groups in scientific research and clinical trials has been a disturbing trend. One particularly troubling aspect is that human **genomic databases** are heavily skewed toward people of European descent. If left unaddressed, this inherent bias will continue to contribute to uneven success rates in so-called precision medicine.

译文 在科学研究和临床试验中，非白人种族的代表性不足一直是一个令人不安的趋势。一个特别棘手的方面是，人类基因组数据库严重偏向欧洲血统的人。如果不加以处理，这种固有的偏见将在所谓的精准医疗中继续导致不均衡的成功率。

背景知识

genomic database：基因组数据库（GDB），为人类基因组计划（HGP）保存和处理基因组图谱数据。GDB 的目标是构建关于人类基因组的百科全书，除了构建基因组图谱之外，还开发了描述序列水平的基因组内容的方法，包括序列变异和其他对功能和表型的描述。

专题二 科技与反思

生词点睛

| **underrepresentation** *n.* 代表性不足 | **disturbing** *adj.* 令人不安的；烦扰的 |
| **genomic** *adj.* 基因组的；染色体的 | **uneven** *adj.* 不均匀的 |

重点表达

❖ contribute to sth. 有助于，促成；是……的原因之一
Plenty of fresh air **contributes to** good health. 多呼吸新鲜空气对健康有益。
Air pollution **contributes to** respiratory diseases. 空气污染会引起呼吸道疾病。

Para. 2 The problem stems from the underlying structure of science. In the early days of genomics, funding for sequencing projects was often highest among mostly white countries, so those populations are better represented in public databases. Also, some minorities have been historically mistreated by scientists—**the Tuskegee syphilis experiment** is one glaring example—and many members of those groups can be understandably reluctant to enter studies.

译文 这个问题源于科学的基本结构。在基因组学的早期，测序项目的资金通常在大多数白人国家中最高，因此这些人口在公共数据库中的代表性就更高。此外，一些少数族裔在历史上一直受到科学家的虐待——塔斯基吉梅毒实验就是一个显著的例子——这些群体中的许多成员不愿参加研究是可以理解的。

背景知识

the Tuskegee syphilis experiment：塔斯基吉梅毒实验，是令不少黑人闻之色变的专有名词，已成为种族主义的代名词之一。自 1932 年起，美国公共卫生部（PHS）以 400 名非洲裔黑人男子为试验品秘密研究梅毒对人体的危害，隐瞒当事人长达 40 年，使大批受害人及其亲属付出了健康乃至生命的代价，人称"塔斯基吉梅毒实验"。

生词点睛

sequence v. 把……按顺序排好	mistreat v. 虐待
glaring adj. 耀眼的；显眼的	reluctant adj. 不情愿的；勉强的

重点表达

❖ stem from 来自，起源于；由……造成
I think my problems **stem from** childhood. 我觉得我的问题源自儿时。

❖ be reluctant to do sth. 不愿做某事
Scarred by the Great Recession, millennials have **been reluctant to** buy a house. 受大萧条的影响，千禧一代们一直不愿买房子。

Para. 3 Early studies were also biased by the types of genetic variation the research focused on. Initially scientists looked at only tiny, single-base-pair DNA differences between populations, ignoring larger variations that were more difficult to assess but that turned out to be more significant than anyone expected. These are now known to cause genetic disease and influence the way drugs are metabolized by different ethnic populations, not just individuals—and advanced technologies allow scientists to identify variations that in many cases have never been seen before.

译文 早期的研究也因所关注的基因变异类型而存在偏见。起初，科学家们只研究了群体间微小的单碱基对的 DNA 差异，而忽略了更大的变异，这些变异更难评估，但结果比任何人预期的都要重要。现在已知这些变异会引起基因疾病，并影响不同种族人群的药物代谢方式，而不仅仅影响个体，而且先进的技术使科学家能够识别出在许多情况下从未见过的变异。

生词点睛

variation n. 变异，变种；变化	assess v. 评定；估价
significant adj. 重要的；重大的	metabolize v. 使新陈代谢；使变形
identify v. 确定；鉴定；识别	

重点表达

❖ focus on 集中注意力/关心于……上
Everybody's eyes were **focused on** her. 大家的视线都集中在她身上。
❖ turn out to be 结果是;原来是
That theory **turns out to be** false. 我们发现那个理论是错误的。

Para. 4 This is an exciting step forward: we are finding that some of these structural differences can explain diseases for which no cause had previously been found—such as **Carney complex**, a rare disorder that causes tumors to appear in various parts of the body, for example, or a mutation that may contribute to bipolar disorder and schizophrenia. And here, too, the effects may well vary from one ethnic group to another.

译文 这是一个令人激动的进步：我们发现这些结构上的差异可以解释以前没有找到病因的疾病，如卡尼综合征，它是一种会导致肿瘤出现在身体的不同部位的罕见疾病，或者说是一种可以导致双向情感障碍和精神分裂症的突变。在这方面，各种病征也可能因种族而异。

背景知识

Carney complex：卡尼综合征（CNC），是一种罕见的遗传性疾病，最早于 1985 年由 J Aidan Carney 首先描述为由粘液瘤、皮肤色素沉着、内分泌功能亢进所组成的综合征。多发性内分泌肿瘤和皮肤损害、心脏累及是本病的基本特点。

生词点睛

structural adj. 结构的；建筑的	**previously** adv. 以前；预先
tumor n. 肿瘤；肿块	**mutation** n. 突变；变化
bipolar adj. 有两极的，双极的	**schizophrenia** n. [内科] 精神分裂症

重点表达

❖ vary from sth. to sth. 因……而异

Now, wild koala population estimates **vary from** 43,000 **to** around 350,000. 现在，野生考拉的数量估计从 43 000 只到大约 350 000 只。

Para. 5 In the field of rare diseases, genome sequencing has proved remarkable at increasing the diagnosis rate, giving answers to patients who might otherwise have gone undiagnosed. Today that approach remains most effective for Caucasian patients because more of their DNA can be interpreted using current genomic data repositories. But as we build up data for people of other ethnicities, we can expect such successes to extend rapidly to patients of any background, which stands to dramatically improve health care for hundreds of millions of people.

译文 在罕见疾病领域，基因组测序已被证明在提高诊断率方面具有显著的作用，为那些原本可能未确诊的患者提供了解决方法。今天，这种方法对白人患者仍然是最有效的，因为他们更多的 DNA 可以通过目前的基因组数据库来解释。但是，随着我们为其他种族的人建立数据，我们就可以预期这样的成功会迅速扩展到任何背景的病人身上，这将极大地改善数亿人的医疗保健。

生词点睛

remarkable *adj*. 显著的；非凡的	**diagnosis** *n*. 诊断
repository *n*. 贮藏室，仓库	**dramatically** *adv*. 显著地；剧烈地

重点表达

❖ hundreds of millions of 数以亿计的

Today, with **hundreds of millions of** people using those products around the world, we are very aware of the trust that you have placed in us, and our responsibility to protect your privacy and data. 今天，世界各地数亿人在使用这些产品，我们非常清楚你们对我们的信任，所以我们有责任保护你们的隐私和数据。

Para. 6 Achieving the vision of precision medicine for individuals of any ethnic group requires more diverse representation in the biological repositories that underlie clinical programs. Advanced DNA-sequencing technology is one tool of many needed to help generate better information about people from all ethnicities for the equitable application of those data in clinical practice.

译文 想要实现为任何种族的个体进行精准医疗的愿景，需要在构成临床项目基础的生物知识库中拥有更多样化的代表。先进的 DNA 测序技术是众多必不可少的工具之一，因为它有助于更好地生成各种族人群的信息，以便在临床实践中公平应用这些数据。

生词点睛

precision *n.* 精确	**diverse** *adj.* 多种多样的；不同的
underlie *v.* 成为……的基础；位于……之下	**advanced** *adj.* 先进的
generate *v.* 使形成；产生	**ethnicity** *n.* 种族地位；种族特点
clinical *adj.* 临床的；诊所的	

词意选选看

1. disturbing ____
2. mistreat ____
3. reluctant ____
4. variation ____
5. remarkable ____
6. diagnosis ____
7. dramatically ____
8. precision ____
9. diverse ____
10. advanced ____

a. 不情愿的
b. 多种多样的；不同的
c. 虐待
d. 显著的；非凡的
e. 显著地；剧烈地
f. 精确
g. 先进的
h. 令人不安的；烦扰的
i. 变异
j. 诊断

·拓展阅读·

基因组数据库

Genomic databases are integral parts of human genome informatics, which enjoyed an exponential growth in the postgenomic era, as a result of the understanding of the genetic etiology of human disorders and the identification of numerous genomic variants. These resources organize this knowledge and variants such that it could be eventually useful not only for molecular diagnosis, but also for clinicians and researchers. Human genomic databases are referred to as online repositories of genomic variants, mainly described for a single or more genes or specifically for a population or ethnic group, aiming to facilitate diagnosis at the DNA level and to correlate genomic variants with specific phenotypic patterns and clinical features.

延伸思考：什么是基因组时代和后基因组时代（the postgenomic era）？

第 6 天

While new technologies like chatbots or artificial intelligence (AI) get a lot of attention, experts at a recent *Guardian* roundtable event, supported by DXC Technology, agreed digital services should be adopted only when they can genuinely make systems more efficient for staff or end users.

The main thing, the panel agreed, is to focus on the end results, rather than processes. "We shouldn't ask how to digitise public services," said Ed Poyntz-Wright, account delivery lead for DXC. "Instead, we should ask how we can use digital technologies to improve services."

Digital technology can also be used behind the scenes, said Maryvonne Hassall, digital director at Aylesbury Vale council, which has developed a number of text and voice-based chatbot services to deal with a wide range of queries. "It's not just about the website," she said. "We use AI internally in customer services to help our agents answer questions. This means people can contact us out of office hours."

Others pointed out several improvements as a result of gathering data. Emma Revie, chief executive of the Trussell Trust, said food banks can now collect data and gain valuable insight, such as showing that the waiting times for universal credit claimants should be cut. Nadira Hussain, director of leadership development and research at Socitm, which represents local government IT managers, said councils have, for instance, made better use of data to tackle problem gambling.

But the panel agreed there are still a number of barriers to creating better digital public services. One is that many people still prefer personal interaction. "We see ambulance services being called out for cases that don't require an ambulance, but a lonely person wants to see a human face," said Vicky Sellick, executive director at charity Nesta. Digital services should be good enough that people want to opt-in.

Another barrier is the need to change the culture of an organisation to make it digitally focused. "That's one of the most challenging things," said an official. "People are attached to their job and the way they've done things… it can be a challenge to get staff to willingly take on new things."

Overcoming digital barriers is necessary as technology is a really fundamental enabler to helping the most vulnerable people, said Lara Sampson, product owner at the Department for Work and Pensions Digital. Digital tools should be the solution to problems and not be used unnecessarily, the panel agreed, and it is important for public organisations not to lose sight of their values, said Jenny Peachey, senior policy and development officer at the Carnegie Trust. Technology must always aim to reduce inequalities and not create more of them.

文章大意

第一段：提出文章中心。
第二段：提出专家组的观点。
第三段：介绍了玛丽冯·哈索尔的观点。
第四段：指出数据收集后应该改进的地方。
第五段：指出数字公共服务仍存在障碍。
第六段：指出数字公共服务的另一个障碍。
第七段：指出克服障碍的必要性。

逐段精讲

Para. 1 While new technologies like chatbots or **artificial intelligence (AI)** get a lot of attention, experts at a recent *Guardian* roundtable event, supported by DXC Technology, agreed digital services should be adopted only when they can genuinely make systems more efficient for staff or end users.

译文 虽然聊天机器人或人工智能（AI）等新技术引起了很多关注，但最近出席了由DXC技术公司赞助的《卫报》圆桌会议的专家认为，只有当数字服务能够真正使系统对员工或终端用户更有效时，才应该被采用。

背景知识

artificial intelligence (AI)：人工智能，英文缩写为 AI。它是研究、开发用于模拟、延伸和扩展人的智能的理论、方法、技术及应用系统的一门新的技术科学。

Guardian：《卫报》是英国的全国性综合内容日报。与《泰晤士报》《每日电讯报》被合称为英国三大报。该报注重报道国际新闻，擅长发表评论和分析性专题文章。

生词点睛

artificial intelligence (AI) 人工智能	adopt *v.* 采用
efficient *adj.* 高效的	

重点表达

❖ **get a lot of attention** 引起了很多关注
Sandy, you **get a lot of attention**, don't you? 山迪，你出大风头了，是吗？

❖ **should be adopted only when...** 只有在……时候，才可以采用
However, diversification should be taken as a last option and **should be adopted only when** the company is very strong financially. 然而，多样化应作为最后一种选择，只有在公司资金非常雄厚的情况下才应被采用。

Para. 2	The main thing, the panel agreed, is to focus on the end results, rather than processes. "We shouldn't ask how to digitise public services," said Ed Poyntz-Wright, account delivery lead for DXC. "Instead, we should ask how we can use digital technologies to improve services."	**译文** 专家组一致认为，目前的主要任务是关注最终结果，而不是过程。"我们不应该问如何将公共服务数字化，"DXC 的账户交付负责人爱德·波因茨·莱特说，"相反，我们应该问如何利用数字技术来改善服务。"

生词点睛

focus on 聚焦，关注	**digitise** *v.* （使）数字化
delivery *n.* 交付；递送	**digital technology** 数字技术

重点表达

❖ rather than 而不是；宁可……也不愿；与其……倒不如

Rather than go straight on to university, why not get some work experience first? 与其直接上大学，为什么不先取得一点工作经验呢？

I always prefer starting early, **rather than** leaving everything to the last minute. 任何事情我总是喜欢早点做，而不是把一切都留到最后一分钟。

Para. 3 Digital technology can also be used behind the scenes, said Maryvonne Hassall, digital director at Aylesbury Vale council, which has developed a number of text and voice-based chatbot services to deal with a wide range of queries. "It's not just about the website," she said. "We use AI internally in customer services to help our agents answer questions. This means people can contact us out of office hours."

译文 艾尔斯伯里谷地方议会的数字主管玛丽冯·哈索尔表示，数字技术也可以在幕后使用，该地方议会已经开发了许多基于文本和语音的聊天机器人服务来处理各种查询。"这不仅仅是关于网站，"她说，"我们在客户服务中使用人工智能来帮助我们的代理商回答问题。这意味着人们可以在非办公时间与我们联系。"

生词点睛

query n. 疑问，询问	customer service 客户服务
contact v. 联系	

重点表达

❖ behind the scenes 在幕后；秘密地

I'd still have a voice **behind the scenes**. 我还是会在幕后指挥。

❖ deal with 处理；对付

They devised proposals to **deal with** air pollution. 他们构想出处理空气污染的方案。

拓 cope with 处理；应付

I hope you're **coping with** it all. 希望你都释然了。

❖ a wide range of 大范围的；各种各样的

Customers have **a wide range of** needs. 客户的需求是多种多样的。

Para. 4 Others pointed out several improvements as a result of gathering data. Emma Revie, chief executive of the **Trussell Trust**, said food banks can now collect data and gain valuable insight, such as showing that the waiting times for universal credit claimants should be cut. Nadira Hussain, director of leadership development and research at Socitm, which represents local government IT managers, said councils have, for instance, made better use of data to tackle problem gambling.

译文 其他人指出了收集数据后一些需要改进的地方。特鲁赛尔信托首席执行官艾玛·里维表示，食品银行现在可以收集数据并获得宝贵的见解，例如表明应该削减普遍信贷申请人的等待时间。再如，纳迪拉·侯赛因是信息技术委员会的领导力发展和研究主管，代表当地政府的IT经理，他表示，地方议会已经更好地利用数据来解决赌博问题。

背景知识

Trussell Trust：特鲁塞尔信托，是一家非政府组织和慈善机构，总部位于英国索尔兹伯里，负责协调该国唯一的全国性食品银行网络。其目标是结束英国的饥饿和贫困，向陷入贫困的人提供紧急粮食和资助。

生词点睛

valuable *adj.* 宝贵的，有用的	**insight** *n.* 洞察力；深刻的见解
claimant *n.* 申请人；索赔人	**tackle** *v.* 应付，处理
gambling *n.* 赌博	

重点表达

❖ point out 指出，指明

I'm missing something obvious you're about to **point out**. 我好像没发现你要指出的重点。

❖ make better use of 更好地利用

The first is to **make better use of** existing competition law. 首先是更好地利用现有的竞争法规。

Para. 5 But the panel agreed there are still a number of barriers to creating better digital public services. One is that many people still prefer personal interaction. "We see ambulance services being called out for cases that don't require an ambulance, but a lonely person wants to see a human face," said Vicky Sellick, executive director at charity **Nesta**. Digital services should be good enough that people want to opt-in.

译文 但专家组一致认为，创建更好的数字公共服务仍存在许多障碍。其中一个是许多人还是更喜欢人际互动。"我们看到一个不需要救护车的病例呼叫了救护车服务，只因一个孤独的人希望看到另一个人的脸庞。"慈善机构 Nesta 执行理事维基·塞利克说。数字服务应该足够好，这样人们才想要选择加入。

背景知识

Nesta：英国国家科学、技术与艺术基金会（NESTA），是一家独立的慈善机构，致力于提高英国的创新能力。该组织通过结合实际计划、投资、政策和研究以及建立合作伙伴关系来采取行动，以促进广泛领域的创新。

生词点睛

barrier n. 障碍	**personal interaction** 人际互动
ambulance n. 救护车	**opt-in** v. 决定加入，选择参加

重点表达

❖ prefer + n. 更喜欢……

Does he **prefer** a particular sort of music? 他有特别喜欢的音乐吗？

Para. 6 Another barrier is the need to change the culture of an organisation to make it digitally focused. "That's one of the most challenging things," said an official. "People are attached to their job and the way they've done things… it can

译文 另一个障碍是需要改变组织的文化，使其以数字化为重点。"这是最具挑战性的事情之一，"一位高级职员说，"人们对自己的工作以及做事的方式有依赖感……让员工自愿

be a challenge to get staff to willingly take on new things."

接受新事物可能是一项挑战。"

生词点睛

challenging *adj.* 富有挑战性的	**attach** *v.* 使依附；使依恋
willingly *adv.* 欣然地；愿意地，乐意地	

重点表达

❖ one of the most + *adj.* + *n.* 最……的之一
It's **one of the most enduring designs** in history. 这是历史上最经久不衰的设计之一。

❖ be attached to 对某事物有感情；依附于
He **is** ardently **attached to** his wife. 他热切地爱着妻子。

Para. 7 Overcoming digital barriers is necessary as technology is a really fundamental enabler to helping the most vulnerable people, said Lara Sampson, product owner at the Department for Work and Pensions Digital. Digital tools should be the solution to problems and not be used unnecessarily, the panel agreed, and it is important for public organisations not to lose sight of their values, said Jenny Peachey, senior policy and development officer at the Carnegie Trust. Technology must always aim to reduce inequalities and not create more of them.

译文 工作和养老金数字部的产品所有者劳拉·桑普森表示，克服数字障碍是必要的，因为技术是帮助最弱势群体的真正基础动力。卡内基信托高级政策和发展官员珍妮·皮奇说，专家组认为，数字工具应该是问题的解决方案，没有必要就不应该使用，公共组织不忽略他们的价值观是很重要的。技术必须始终致力于减少不平等，而不是制造更多的不平等。

生词点睛

overcome v. 克服	fundamental adj. 根本的；基本的；基础的
enabler n. 使能器，使能者；促成者	inequality n. 不平等
vulnerable adj. 易受攻击的；易受伤害的；有弱点的	

重点表达

❖ lose sight of 忽略；不再看见

I think you're **losing sight of** the big picture here. 我认为你们没有看清大局。

❖ aim to do sth. 旨在做某事

Musk has made clear he's **aiming to** do away with workers. 马斯克已经明确表示，他的目标是替代工人。

词意选选看

1. adopt _____
2. efficient _____
3. improve _____
4. deal with _____
5. valuable _____
6. overcome _____
7. fundamental _____
8. barrier _____
9. vulnerable _____
10. opt-in _____

a. 宝贵的，有用的
b. 克服
c. 高效的
d. 易受伤害的
e. 改善
f. 采用
g. 根本的；基本的
h. 决定加入，选择参加
i. 处理
j. 障碍

拓展阅读

数字服务税

  U.S. Treasury Secretary Steven Mnuchin has urged all countries to suspend the introduction of digital service taxes as nations work towards a multilateral deal on international taxation. The United States firmly opposes digital service taxes because they have a discriminatory impact on U.S.-based businesses and are inconsistent with the architecture of current international tax rules, which seek to tax net income rather than gross revenues.

延伸思考：数字服务税的实施前景如何？

第 7 天

It is a movement building steady momentum: a call to make research data, software code and experimental methods publicly available and transparent. A spirit of openness is gaining traction in the science community, and is the only way, say advocates, to address a "crisis" in science whereby too few findings are successfully reproduced. Furthermore, they say, it is the best way for researchers to gather the range of observations that are necessary to speed up discoveries or to identify large-scale trends.

The open-data shift poses a conundrum for junior researchers, who are carving out their niche. On the one hand, the drive to share is gathering official steam. Since 2013, global scientific bodies—including the European Commission, the US Office of Science and Technology Policy and the Global Research Council—have begun to back policies that support increased public access to research.

On the other hand, scientists disagree about how much and when they should share data, and they debate whether sharing it is more likely to accelerate science and make it more robust, or to introduce vulnerabilities and problems.

As more journals and funders adopt data-sharing requirements, and as a growing number of enthusiasts call for more openness, junior researchers must find their place between adopters and those who continue to hold out, even as they strive to launch their own careers.

One key challenge facing young scientists is how to be open without becoming scientifically vulnerable. They must determine the risk of jeopardizing a job offer or a collaboration proposal from those who are wary of—or unfamiliar with—open science. And they must learn how to capitalize on the movement's benefits, such as opportunities for more citations and a way to build a reputation without the need for conventional metrics, such as publication in high-impact journals.

And although there is a time cost associated with uploading and organizing raw data, subsequent queries can often be averted by adding reader-friendly instructions at the start. An astronomer recommends that researchers simultaneously upload tutorials and examples of how to use the content.

In the end, sharing data, software and materials with colleagues can help an early-career researcher to obtain recognition—a crucial component of success. "The thing you are searching for is reputation," says Titus Brown, a genomics researcher at the University of California, Davis. "To get grants and jobs, you have to be relevant and achieve some level of public recognition. Anything you do that advances your presence—especially in a larger sphere, outside the communities you know—is a net win."

文章大意

第一段：引出数据共享这个主题并阐述这一行动的积极意义。
第二段：说明数据共享这一行动正得到官方的支持。
第三段：介绍了科学家对数据共享的考虑及争论点。
第四段：说明初级研究员必须做出抉择。
第五段：介绍了年轻科学家面临的挑战及应对措施。
第六段：介绍了如何使原始数据更方便读者使用。
第七段：总结并引用别人的话说明：初级研究员应该接受这一转变。

逐段精讲

Para. 1 It is a movement building steady momentum: a call to make research data, software code and experimental methods publicly available and transparent. A spirit of openness is gaining traction in the science community, and is the only way, say advocates, to address a "crisis" in science whereby too few findings are successfully reproduced. Furthermore, they say, it is the best way for researchers to gather the range of observations that are necessary to speed up discoveries or to identify large-scale trends.

译文 这是一个建立稳定势头的变化：呼吁将研究数据、软件代码和实验方法公开化和透明化。一种开放的精神正在科学界变得越来越有魅力，倡导者说，能被成功复制的研究成果太少了，这是解决这一科学"危机"的唯一途径。此外，他们说，对于研究人员来说，这是收集评论的最佳方式，这些评论是加速研究发现或确定大规模趋势所必需的。

生词点睛

momentum *n.* 推进力；动力	**transparent** *adj.* 透明的
traction *n.* 魅力；吸引力	**advocate** *n.* 支持者；提倡者
address *v.* 解决；处理	**finding** *n.* 调查发现；调研结果
reproduce *v.* 复制，重现	**observation** *n.*（尤指据所见、所闻、所读而作的）评论

重点表达

❖ it is the best way for sb. to do sth. 做某事对某人来说是最佳方式

As a big developing agricultural country, **it is the best way for China to** dispose sludge through forest application. 对我国这样一个发展中的农业大国来说，利用森林资源处置污泥是最佳办法。

Para. 2 The open-data shift poses a conundrum for junior researchers, who are carving out their niche. On the one hand, the drive to share is gathering official steam. Since 2013, global scientific bodies—including the **European Commission**, the **US Office of Science and Technology Policy** and the **Global Research Council**—have begun to back policies that support increased public access to research.

译文 开放数据这一转变给正在开拓自己职业生涯的初级研究员带来了一个难题。一方面，数据共享这一行动正得到官方的支持。自2013年以来，包括欧盟委员会、美国白宫科技政策办公室和全球研究理事会在内的全球科研机构已经开始支持增加公众获得研究结果的机会的政策。

背景知识

European Commission：欧盟委员会，简称欧委会，是欧洲联盟的常设执行机构，也是欧盟唯一有权起草法令的机构。

the US Office of Science and Technology Policy：美国白宫科技政策办公室（OSTP），是美国于1976年根据《国家科学技术政策、组织和优先领域法案》成立的，设在总统行政办公室之内，主要职责是：就相关事项向总统提供科学、及时的建议，确保行政机构的政策符合科学规律，协调行政机构的科技工作。

the Global Research Council：全球研究理事会（GRC），由美国国家科学基金会、德国科学基金会和中国科学院等 11 家机构发起，于 2012 年创立。作为非官方科学组织，GRC 旨在探讨和寻求国际科技界能够共同接受的科学发展方略，推动和实现更多、更好的国际科技合作。

生词点睛

conundrum *n*. 令人迷惑的难题；复杂难解的问题	**junior** *adj*. 职位低的，初级的
niche *n*. 壁龛；合适的职业	**gather steam**（计划、观念等）逐渐变得重要，逐渐得到关注
back *v*. 帮助；支持	

重点表达

❖ **carve out a niche** 凭自身努力获得一席之地

Advanced production process, superior quality and reasonable price enable us to **carve out a niche** amid the keen market competition. 先进的生产工艺、优越的质量和合理的价格使我们能够在激烈的市场竞争中占有一席之地。

Para. 3 On the other hand, scientists disagree about how much and when they should share data, and they debate whether sharing it is more likely to accelerate science and make it more robust, or to introduce vulnerabilities and problems.

译文 另一方面，科学家们对他们应该在多大程度上以及什么时候共享数据存在分歧，同时他们还在争论，数据共享是更有可能加速科学的发展，使其更强劲，还是会带来漏洞和问题。

生词点睛

accelerate *v*.（使）加速，加快	**robust** *adj*. 强劲的；富有活力的
introduce *v*. 使（新事物）开始	**vulnerability** *n*. 弱点；脆弱性

重点表达

❖ **disagree about** 在……方面意见不统一；对……意见不一

Not only are they divided about where the economy is headed, they even **disagree about** how it is faring today. 他们不但对经济的走势持不同意见，甚至连目前经济处于何种状态都无法统一观点。

Para. 4 As more journals and funders adopt data-sharing requirements, and as a growing number of enthusiasts call for more openness, junior researchers must find their place between adopters and those who continue to hold out, even as they strive to launch their own careers.

译文 随着越来越多的期刊和资助者接受数据共享的要求，以及越来越多的支持者呼吁提高开放度，初级研究员必须在采用者和继续坚持下去的人之间找到自己的位置，即使他们在努力开创自己的事业。

生词点睛

enthusiast *n.* 热烈支持者；热情赞成者

重点表达

❖ **a growing number of** 越来越多的

As weather cools across the United States, **a growing number of** Americans visit farms. 随着美国各地天气变冷，越来越多的美国人到农场参观。

❖ **hold out** 维持；坚持

They can't **hold out** much longer. 他们坚持不了多久。

❖ **strive to do sth.** 设法；努力做好

Eisenhower **strove to** avoid war at any cost. 艾森豪威尔不惜一切代价阻止战争的发生。

❖ **launch one's career** 开始某人的职业生涯

College students are ready to **launch their careers**. 大学毕业生准备开启他们的职业生涯。

专题二　科技与反思

Para. 5 One key challenge facing young scientists is how to be open without becoming scientifically vulnerable. They must determine the risk of jeopardizing a job offer or a collaboration proposal from those who are wary of—or unfamiliar with—open science. And they must learn how to capitalize on the movement's benefits, such as opportunities for more citations and a way to build a reputation without the need for conventional metrics, such as publication in high-impact journals.

译文　年轻科学家面临的一个关键挑战是如何开放数据，而又不会对自己的科研产生不利影响。他们必须确定那些对开放科学持谨慎态度或不熟悉开放科学的人提出的工作邀请或合作建议可能造成危害的风险。他们还必须学会利用这一转变的好处，比如获得更多被引用的机会，以及在不需要常规指标（例如在影响力很大的期刊上发表作品）的情况下建立声誉的方法。

生词点睛

jeopardize *v.* 危及，损害	**collaboration** *n.* 合作，协作
citation *n.* 引用；引证	**metric** *n.* 度量标准

重点表达

❖ be wary of 提防；当心
They may **be wary of** unexpected visitors. 他们恐怕不会欢迎不速之客。

❖ capitalize on sth. 充分利用某事物；从某事物中获利
Nobody's figured out a way to **capitalize on** an impact site that isn't visible. 谁也没有想出个办法来利用那个已经看不见的撞击现场。

Para. 6 And although there is a time cost associated with uploading and organizing raw data, subsequent queries can often be averted by adding reader-friendly instructions at the start. An astronomer recommends that researchers simultaneously upload tutorials and examples of how to use the content.

译文　尽管上传和组织原始数据有一定的时间成本，但是随后可以通过在一开始添加方便读者的指令来避免随后的查询。一位天文学家建议研究人员同时上传如何使用这些内容的教程和示例。

087

生词点睛

upload *v.* 上载，上传	**raw data** 原始（未处理的）数据
subsequent *adj.* 后来的；随后的	**avert** *v.* 防止，避免
recommend *v.* 推荐	**simultaneously** *adv.* 同时地
tutorial *n.* 教程；使用说明书	

重点表达

❖ be averted by 被避免

Many traffic accidents can **be averted by** courtesy. 文明驾驶可以防止很多事故的发生。

Para. 7 In the end, sharing data, software and materials with colleagues can help an early-career researcher to obtain recognition—a crucial component of success. "The thing you are searching for is reputation," says Titus Brown, a genomics researcher at the University of California, Davis. "To get grants and jobs, you have to be relevant and achieve some level of public recognition. Anything you do that advances your presence—especially in a larger sphere, outside the communities you know—is a net win."

译文 最后，与同事分享数据、软件和材料可以帮助初级研究员获得认可——这是成功的一个重要组成部分。"你所追求的是名誉，"加州大学戴维斯分校的基因组学研究人员提图斯·布朗说，"要获得资助和工作，你必须具备相关经验，并受到一定程度的公众认可。你所做的任何能提高你知名度的事情——尤其是在一个更大的领域，一个你不知道的领域——都具有极大的优势。"

生词点睛

component *n.* 组成部分；成分	**genomics** *n.* 基因组学
grant *n.* （政府、机构的）拨款	**sphere** *n.* 范围；领域

词意选选看

1. transparent ____
2. traction ____
3. accelerate ____
4. robust ____
5. simultaneously ____
6. jeopardize ____
7. metric ____
8. avert ____
9. tutorial ____
10. grant ____

a. 强劲的；富有活力的
b.（政府、机构的）拨款
c. 教程；使用说明书
d. 防止，避免
e. 度量标准
f. 透明的
g. 魅力；吸引力
h. 同时地
i. 危及，损害
j.（使）加速，加快

拓展阅读

数据共享面临的问题

Group data sharing in cloud environments has become a hot topic in recent decades. With the popularity of cloud computing, how to achieve secure and efficient data sharing in cloud environments is an urgent problem to be solved. In addition, how to achieve both anonymity and traceability is also a challenge in the cloud for data sharing.

延伸思考：数据共享有哪些分类？数据共享有何利弊？

第 8 天

In the United Kingdom, the time young people spend online has almost doubled over the past decade, the communications-industry regulator, Ofcom, has found. Parental concerns about media use are rising, too—fuelled by headlines and political pronouncements. On 2 October, 2018, Matt Hancock, UK Secretary of State for Health, issued an urgent warning, saying that the threat to children's mental health from social media is similar to that from sugar to their physical health.

Current evidence for an association between digital-technology use and adolescent well-being is contradictory and comes mainly from household panel surveys and other large-scale social polls, with thousands to millions of respondents. The questions represent a compromise between usefulness and not placing too much burden on respondents. They are simplified, are not standardized and often do not map straightforwardly onto the validated instruments that clinical or social scientists use to measure constructs such as "well-being" and "technology use".

A study published this week in *Nature Human Behaviour* introduces a different approach. The authors examine three key large-scale data sets, two from the United States and one from the United Kingdom, that include information about teenager well-being, digital-technology use and a host of other variables. Instead of running one or a handful of statistical analyses, they run all theoretically plausible analyses (combinations of dependent and independent variables, with or without co-variates)—in the case of one data set, more than 40,000. This allows the authors to map how the association between digital-technology use and well-being can vary—from negative to non-significant to positive—depending on how the same data set is used.

The authors' overall calculations did find a statistically significant negative association between technology use and well-being: more screen time is associated with lower well-being in the young people surveyed. But the effects are so small—explaining at only 0.4% of the variation in well-being—as to be of little practical value.

To put this into context, the authors also looked at the associations between well-being and a range of other variables, such as binge drinking, being bullied, smoking, getting enough sleep, eating breakfast, eating vegetables, wearing glasses or going to the cinema. Well-being was more strongly associated, either positively or negatively, with most of these other variables than with digital-technology use. In fact, regularly eating potatoes was almost as negatively associated with well-being as was technology use, and the negative association between wearing glasses and wellbeing was greater.

This article is hardly the final word: its conclusions rely on the examination of associations, rather than on potential causal relationships. However, it does suggest that dire warnings are not warranted. And it is a reminder that limited evidence can distort public discourse when the issue is of pervasive significance—such as when parental decisions and the health of children are involved. This is also the conclusion reached by the UK Royal College of Paediatrics and Child Health, in guidance on the health effects of screen time that it issued earlier this month.

文章大意

第一段：指出社交媒体的使用会危害儿童的心理健康。
第二段：数字技术的使用与青少年幸福感之间的关联的现有证据是矛盾的。
第三段：介绍了一种新的研究方法。
第四段：调查发现年轻人面对电子屏幕的时间越长，幸福感越低。
第五段：研究了幸福感与生活中其他变量之间的关系。
第六段：总结全文，以上研究未能得出结论。

逐段精讲

Para. 1 In the United Kingdom, the time young people spend online has almost doubled over the past decade, the communications-industry regulator, Ofcom, has found. Parental concerns about media use are rising, too—fuelled by headlines and political pronouncements. On 2 October, 2018, Matt Hancock, UK Secretary of State for Health, issued an urgent warning, saying that the threat to children's mental health from social media is similar to that from sugar to their physical health.

译文 通信行业监管机构 Ofcom 发现，在英国，年轻人上网的时间在过去十年几乎翻了一番。家长们对媒体使用的担忧越来越强烈，新闻头条和政治声明更加剧了这种情况。2018年10月2日，英国卫生大臣马特·汉考克发布紧急警告称，社交媒体对儿童心理健康的威胁与糖对儿童身体健康的威胁类似。

生词点睛

concern *n.* 担心，忧虑	**fuel** *v.* 刺激；使更强烈
pronouncement *n.* 公告，声明	**urgent** *adj.* 紧迫的，急迫的；紧要的
mental health 心理健康	**physical health** 身体健康

重点表达

❖ **be concerned about** 对……表示担心/忧虑

He doesn't **seem concerned about** his health. 他好像对自己的健康毫不关心。

❖ **be similar to** 与……相似

I've discovered that their journeys **were similar to** mine. 我发现他们的经历与我的相似。

Para. 2 Current evidence for an association between digital-technology use and adolescent well-being is contradictory and comes mainly from household panel surveys and other large-scale social polls, with thousands to millions of respondents. The questions represent a compromise between usefulness and not placing too much burden on respondents. They are simplified, are not standardized and often do not map straightforwardly onto the validated instruments that clinical or social scientists use to measure constructs such as "well-being" and "technology use".

译文 数字技术的使用与青少年幸福感之间的关联的现有证据是矛盾的，这些证据主要来自家庭小组调查和其他大规模的社会调查，参与社会调查的对象有数千甚至数百万名。这些问题既考虑到了有用性，又没有给受访者增加太大的负担。这些问题被简化了，但没有标准化，而且通常和有效仪器没有直接关系，临床或社会科学家会用这些仪器来衡量"幸福感"和"技术使用"等概念。

生词点睛

well-being *n.* 健康，幸福	**contradictory** *adj.* 矛盾的
respondent *n.* 调查对象；答卷人	**compromise** *n.* 折中，妥协
straightforwardly *adv.* 直截了当地；正直地	

重点表达

❖ **place too much burden on sb.** 给某人增加太大的负担

It is not advisable to **place too much burden on** high school students. 给高中生增加太大负担是不可取的。

Para. 3 A study published this week in *Nature Human Behaviour* introduces a different approach. The authors examine three key large-scale data sets, two from the United States and one from the United Kingdom, that include information about teenager well-being, digital-technology use and a host of other variables. Instead of running one or a handful of statistical analyses, they run all theoretically plausible analyses (combinations of dependent and independent variables, with or without co-variates)—in the case of one data set, more than 40,000. This allows the authors to map how the association between digital-technology use and well-being can vary—from negative to non-significant to positive—depending on how the same data set is used.

译文 本周发表于《自然人类行为》的一项研究介绍了一种与众不同的方法。作者研究了三个关键的大规模数据集,其中两个来自美国,一个来自英国,数据集包括有关青少年幸福感、数字技术使用和许多其他变量的信息。研究人员没有进行一个或几个统计分析,而是在一个容量超过40 000的数据集中进行了所有理论上的合理分析(将因变量和自变量进行组合,添加或去掉协变量)。这使得作者能够绘制数字技术使用与幸福感之间的关系的变化情况——从负面到不重要再到正面——取决于如何使用相同的数据集。

生词点睛

variable n. [数]变量;可变因素	**a handful of** 几个人(物),少数人(物)
significant adj. 重要的	**plausible** adj. 貌似有理的;似乎是真的
map v. 绘制……的地图	

重点表达

❖ **a host of** 许多

A host of memories appear when you hear a word you remember. 当你听到你记得的字词时,许多记忆会浮现。

❖ **depend on** 取决于；依赖；依靠

You may **depend on** the accuracy of the report. 你可以信赖报告的准确性。

Much will also **depend on** the attitude of the actor themselves. 很多事情也将取决于演员自己的态度。

Para. 4 The authors' overall calculations did find a statistically significant negative association between technology use and well-being: more screen time is associated with lower well-being in the young people surveyed. But the effects are so small—explaining at only 0.4% of the variation in well-being—as to be of little practical value.

译文 作者的整体计算确实发现技术的使用与幸福感之间在统计学上呈现负相关：根据调查，年轻人面对电子屏幕的时间越长，幸福感越低。但这一因素的影响是很小的——在影响幸福感变化的因素中只占 0.4%——实用价值也比较小。

生词点睛

calculation n. 计算	screen time 屏幕时间
practical value 实用价值	

重点表达

❖ **be associated with** 和……联系在一起；与……有关

You might not expect such a frightening dream to **be associated with** something joyful. 你大概不会想到把这么可怕的梦和快乐的事联系起来。

Para. 5 To put this into context, the authors also looked at the associations between well-being and a range of other variables, such as binge drinking, being bullied, smoking, getting enough sleep, eating breakfast, eating vegetables, wearing glasses or going to the cinema. Well-being was more strongly associated, either positively or negatively, with most of these other

译文 为了将这一点纳入背景，作者还研究了幸福感与一系列其他变量之间的关系，如酗酒、被欺负、吸烟、睡眠充足、吃早餐、吃蔬菜、戴眼镜或去电影院。幸福感与大多数其他变量的正相关或负相关关系要比与数字技术使用

variables than with digital-technology use. In fact, regularly eating potatoes was almost as negatively associated with well-being as was technology use, and the negative association between wearing glasses and wellbeing was greater.

之间的关系更密切。事实上，经常吃土豆几乎和技术使用一样与幸福感呈负相关，戴眼镜与幸福感之间的负相关性更大。

生词点睛

| binge drinking 纵酒狂饮 | bully v. 欺负，恐吓 |

重点表达

❖ in fact 事实上

In fact, in some ways, our learning path has only just begun. 事实上，在某些方面，我们的学习之路才刚刚开始。

The rumour is without foundation **in fact**. 这个谣传没有事实根据。

Para. 6 This article is hardly the final word: its conclusions rely on the examination of associations, rather than on potential causal relationships. However, it does suggest that dire warnings are not warranted. And it is a reminder that limited evidence can distort public discourse when the issue is of pervasive significance—such as when parental decisions and the health of children are involved. This is also the conclusion reached by the UK Royal College of Paediatrics and Child Health, in guidance on the health effects of screen time that it issued earlier this month.

译文 本文很难说是最后的结论：它的结论依赖于对相关性的检验，而不是潜在的因果关系。然而，它确实表明，可怕的警告是没有必要的。这提醒我们，当这个问题具有普遍意义时，例如涉及父母的决定和儿童的健康时，不充足的证据会扭曲公共言论。这也是英国皇家儿科及儿童健康学院在本月早些时候发布的关于屏幕时间对健康的影响的指南中得出的结论。

生词点睛

dire *adj.* 可怕的	**warranted** *adj.* 保证的；担保的
distort *v.* 扭曲	**public discourse** 公共言论
pervasive *adj.* 到处存在的，普遍的	**guidance** *n.* 指导，指南
issue *v.* 发布	

重点表达

❖ it is a reminder that... 这是一个提醒……

It is a reminder that we need to care about the world we live in and that we should learn to respect life and nature. 这是一个提醒：我们需要关心我们居住的世界，并且我们应该学会尊重生命和大自然。

❖ be of + *adj.* + significance 有……意义的

It could **be of great significance** to boost economic ties and political ties. 这对促进经济联系和政治关系具有重大意义。

拓 be of no significance 无关紧要

It **is of no significance** whether you go or not. 你去不去都无关紧要。

❖ reach a conclusion 得出结论；达成一个结论

She saw at once that Ned had **reached a** very different **conclusion**. 她立即明白奈德已然下了个截然相反的结论。

词意选选看

1. fuel _____
2. pronouncement _____
3. mental health _____
4. well-being _____
5. contradictory _____
6. compromise _____
7. significant _____
8. plausible _____

a. 妥协
b. 重要的
c. 扭曲
d. 貌似有理的
e. 心理健康
f. 普遍的
g. 声明
h. 刺激

9. distort ____
10. pervasive ____

i. 幸福
j. 矛盾的

拓展阅读

数字屏幕的使用

　　Digital screen use is a staple of contemporary life for adults and children, whether they are browsing on laptops and smartphones, or watching TV. Paediatricians and scientists have long expressed concerns about the impact of overusing technology on people's well-being. However, new Oxford University research suggests that existing guidance managing children's digital media time may not be as beneficial as first thought.

延伸思考：如何有效地控制孩子的屏幕时间？

专题三

企业与社会

导 言

作为社会生产活动的核心载体，企业一直是各大报刊评论员关注的焦点，企业类话题同样是每年考研英语阅读中必考的重点。接下来笔者将结合企业负有的几种核心责任，来介绍考研英语阅读中关于企业类话题的考查角度：

第一，对自身而言，企业负有赚取利润这一最根本的责任。故考研英语真题中有很多为陷入困境、危机中的企业进行症结分析、提出经营改进意见的文章。

第二，企业对其员工负有责任。如何保证员工的福利待遇、提高员工的工作效率是企业管理的一个核心课题，相关的企业类文章经常作为考研英语二的阅读真题出现。

第三，企业对消费者负有责任。企业应该尽可能地向消费者提供物美价廉的产品以及服务，并保证其售前与售后的权益。这种愿景的典型对立面是以暴利著称的金融公司以及滥用用户数据的科技巨头，此两类企业一直是考研英语阅读中的重点批判对象。

第四，企业对政府负有责任。企业需要保证其经营的合法性以及合规性，并配合政府的监督行为以及必要的干预行为。从这方面来看，考研英语阅读中既有批判个别企业的违规行为的文章，又有为政府的市场监管出谋划策的文章。

第五，企业对社会负有责任。一方面，企业在生产过程中会造成环境污染，固然应该肩负起相应的环境治理责任。另一方面，企业输出的产品会对社会的发展产生潜移默化的影响，这在拥有巨大影响力的新闻传媒企业身上体现得尤为明显，故企业应该竭力避免对社会产生负面的导向作用。

综上所述，企业负有多方面的重大责任，而重担之下，任何企业都难免有所疏漏，因此考研英语阅读真题中凡是涉及企业的话题几乎全都以批评为主。其中"出镜"最多的就是上文中提到的金融公司、科技巨头和新闻传媒三类企业，本专题也选取了相关的文章，希望有助于加深考研学子们对这一话题的了解。

2010—2021年相关考研英语阅读真题

英语一

2012　Text-2　安特吉公司之罪
2015　Text-4　新闻公司中的道德问题
2016　Text-3　企业社会责任与其商业价值
2016　Text-4　《纽约时报》的转型

2018　Text-3　科技巨头与公众数据垄断
2019　Text-1　企业经营中的长期主义
2020　Text-4　法国制裁科技巨头
2021　Text-1　铁路公司票价上涨
2021　Text-4　宽带供应商垄断和网络中立性问题

英语二

2010　Text-3　商业广告与习惯养成
2011　Text-1　独立董事的重要性
2011　Text-2　美国报业的衰退
2012　Text-2　色彩认知与市场营销
2018　Text-3　科技巨头滥用用户信息
2018　Text-4　深度工作的诀窍
2020　Text-2　CEO 的高薪之因
2021　Text-3　科技巨头并购初创企业

第 1 天

We hear it said all the time: "Technology will save us." The sentiment is so prevalent that it even led to a dispute with a startup of a similar name. But in an era dominated by the "big four" (Google, Amazon, Facebook and Apple) the idea that tech will save us rings hollow, an example of utopian messaging being used to conceal the simple pursuit of profit.

Having proposed solutions to everything from food shortages to suicide prevention to climate breakdown, companies such as Google and Facebook—two of the leading western companies in the artificial intelligence arms race—claim there's almost nothing that cannot be tackled through tech. But there are reasons to be skeptical. These companies' business models depend on the development of ever more complex algorithms, sustained by enormous quantities of data. This data is used to improve the algorithms—but access to it is also sold to advertisers and third-party businesses.

It also neglects to mention that unprecedented access to our critical infrastructure and publicly generated data would be given to a US tech giant. The collaboration between DeepMind and the privatised National Grid has for now been abandoned for reasons that are unclear. A recent article in *Forbes* speculates that the two companies couldn't reach an agreement on costs and intellectual property rights, in perhaps the most telling example of big tech's ambitions to boost revenues through the commandeering of national infrastructure. Could Google's recent engagement with BT be built on a similar ambition?

Giving tech giants the power to "solve" social problems would mean granting them an immense stake in almost everything that our society requires in order to function. Google is currently signing contracts with the NHS to process patient records, despite there being legal question marks over a similar arrangement with a London hospital a few years ago. What's more, the climate crisis is a political, not a technological problem. Whatever improvements Google or Facebook could make to our infrastructure would still fall far short of solving it. And when environmental collapse stands to affect poorest communities the hardest, the question remains as to how an industry that drives extreme wealth inequality can really be said to help build a greener, more humane, world.

These companies are able to make it seem as though their sole ambition is to optimise and improve their systems for the greater good. But this rhetoric distracts us from the fact that they are ushering in a new kind of "surveillance capitalism", whereby a small number of entities extract enormous amounts of wealth through their access to data that is generated by us, the public.

文章大意

第一段:"科技拯救人类"的说法是科技巨头掩盖其逐利本质的说辞。

第二、三段:科技巨头们在解决越来越多的公共问题的同时也获取了越来越多的数据并将其转卖。几个企业与政府的合作都因利益问题而失败,从中能看出企业的目的就是营利。

第四段:科技企业在越发深入参与解决社会问题治理的同时,得以从社会运行的各个领域获取利益。科技并不能解决像气候危机这样的政治问题,也无法解决自身带来的财富不平等问题。

第五段:科技巨头正在走向"监控资本主义",通过社会产生的数据来获取巨额财富。

逐段精讲

Para. 1 We hear it said all the time: "Technology will save us." The sentiment is so prevalent that it even led to a dispute with a startup of a similar name. But in an era dominated by the "big four" (Google, Amazon, Facebook and Apple) the idea that tech will save us rings hollow, an example of utopian messaging being used to conceal the simple pursuit of profit.

译文 我们总能听到这样的说法:"科技拯救人类。"这种情绪非常普遍,甚至引发了一场关于同名创业公司的争论。但在一个由"四大(科技巨头)"(谷歌、亚马逊、脸书和苹果)主导的时代,科技拯救人类这一理念显得很虚伪,因为他们在用乌托邦式的理念掩饰其逐利的本质。

生词点睛

sentiment *n.* 情绪	**startup** *n.* 创业公司
utopian *adj.* 乌托邦的；理想化的	**conceal** *v.* 掩盖；隐藏

重点表达

❖ (sth.) **ring hollow** 某种说法是空谈

His promises always **ring hollow.** 他的种种承诺都是空话。

Para. 2 Having proposed solutions to everything from food shortages to suicide prevention to climate breakdown, companies such as Google and Facebook—two of the leading western companies in the artificial intelligence arms race—claim there's almost nothing that cannot be tackled through tech. But there are reasons to be skeptical. These companies' business models depend on the development of ever more complex algorithms, sustained by enormous quantities of data. This data is used to improve the algorithms—but access to it is also sold to advertisers and third-party businesses.

译文 从食品短缺到自杀干预再到气候危机，针对各种问题，谷歌和脸书这两个在人工智能研发竞赛中领军的西方企业都给出了解决方案；这些公司声称，基本没有科技解决不了的事情。但我们有理由对此表示怀疑。这些企业的商业模式依赖于越发复杂的算法的进步，而这种进步则需要无数的数据来支撑。这些数据被用来改善算法，但数据的访问权同时也被卖给了广告商和第三方企业。

生词点睛

propose *v.* 提出（建议）	**suicide prevention** 自杀干预
arms race 军备竞赛	**skeptical** *adj.* 怀疑的
business model 商业模式	**enormous** *adj.* 不计其数的

重点表达

❖ **ever more** + *adj.* 越发……的

They are promoting their products with **ever more extravagant** claims. 他们推销产品时的说法越来越夸张离谱了。

Para. 3 It also neglects to mention that unprecedented access to our critical infrastructure and publicly generated data would be given to a US tech giant. The collaboration between DeepMind and the privatised National Grid has for now been abandoned for reasons that are unclear. A recent article in *Forbes* speculates that the two companies couldn't reach an agreement on costs and intellectual property rights, in perhaps the most telling example of big tech's ambitions to boost revenues through the commandeering of national infrastructure. Could Google's recent engagement with **BT** be built on a similar ambition?

译文 同样被避而不提的是，美国的一家科技巨头将会得到英国关键基础设施以及公共数据的前所未有的访问权限。DeepMind 以及私企美国电网公司的合作目前已经因为某些未知原因被叫停了。《福布斯》杂志近期的一篇文章怀疑，两家公司无法达成共识可能是因为费用和知识产权问题，这充分体现了大型科技公司试图通过掌控国家基础设施来实现创收的野心。谷歌与英国电信集团最近的合作是否也是出于同样的目的呢？

背景知识

BT：英国电信集团（British Telecom），原为英国国营电信公用事业，由英国邮政总局管理，1981 年 10 月 1 日脱离英国皇家邮政，变成独立的国营事业。

生词点睛

unprecedented *adj.* 前所未有的	**giant** *n.* 巨头
grid *n.* 输电网；网格	**speculate** *v.* 推测
intellectual property rights 知识产权	**telling** *adj.* 显著的
boost *v.* 增加	**commandeer** *v.* 强行征用
engagement *n.* 约定；订婚	

重点表达

❖ reach an agreement on sth. 就某事达成一致意见

Politicians failed to **reach an agreement on** a new prime minister after three days of intense debate. 经过长达三天的激烈讨论，政治家们仍未能就由谁出任新总理一事达成共识。

Para. 4 Giving tech giants the power to "solve" social problems would mean granting them an immense stake in almost everything that our society requires in order to function. Google is currently signing contracts with the **NHS** to process patient records, despite there being legal question marks over a similar arrangement with a London hospital a few years ago. What's more, the climate crisis is a political, not a technological problem. Whatever improvements Google or Facebook could make to our infrastructure would still fall far short of solving it. And when environmental collapse stands to affect poorest communities the hardest, the question remains as to how an industry that drives extreme wealth inequality can really be said to help build a greener, more humane, world.

译文 赋予科技巨头们"解决"社会问题的权力就意味着，这些企业可以从社会赖以运行的几乎每个领域中都分到一大块利益蛋糕。目前谷歌正在与英国国家医疗服务体系签订协议以获取患者记录，尽管几年前其与伦敦医院签订类似的协议时就曾一度引发法律争论。此外，气候危机是个政治问题而非技术问题。所以无论谷歌或脸书能给我们的基础设施系统带来怎样的改善，都远不足以解决气候问题。而当那些最贫困的地方即将面临环境破坏所带来的最糟糕的影响时，我们又怎么能说那些造成了财富极端不平等的企业帮我们建立了一个更加环保、更加人道的世界呢？

背景知识

NHS：英国国家医疗服务体系（National Health Service），承担着保障英国全民公费医疗保健的重任，其经费来源于税收，由英国政府统一管理。凡有收入的英国公民都必须参加英国国家医疗服务体系，不管他们收入多少，都按统一的标准缴纳保险费，也按统一的标准享受有关福利。

生词点睛

immense *adj.* 巨大的	**stake** *n.* 股份；利益
process *v.* 加工；处理	**collapse** *n.* 倒塌；崩塌
stand to do 准备；即将	**drive** *v.* 导致；推动
inequality *n.* 不平等	**humane** *adj.* 人道的；仁慈的

重点表达

❖ whatever 引导名词性从句

I will forgive **whatever** mistakes you make. 我会原谅你犯的任何错误。

拓 whatever 引导状语从句

Whatever mistakes you make, I will forgive you. 无论你犯了什么错误，我都会原谅你。

❖ fall short of 不足以；达不到

I feel that my ability **falls short of** my wishes. 我感到力不从心。

Para. 5 These companies are able to make it seem as though their sole ambition is to optimise and improve their systems for the greater good. But this rhetoric distracts us from the fact that they are ushering in a new kind of "surveillance capitalism", whereby a small number of entities extract enormous amounts of wealth through their access to data that is generated by us, the public.

译文 这些公司让自己看上去只是为了更崇高的利益而优化和改善其系统。但这种论调使人们忽视了他们正在走向新型"监控资本主义"的事实，一小部分人能通过获取人民大众产生的数据来汲取大量的财富。

生词点睛

sole *adj.* 唯一的	**optimise** *v.* 优化
distract *v.* 使分心	**usher** *v.* 引导；引向
surveillance *n.* 监控	**entity** *n.* 主体；实体

重点表达

❖ for the greater good 为了更崇高的利益

Victims want to see justice done not just for themselves, but **for the greater good** of society. 受害者希望正义得到伸张，这不仅是为了他们自己，也是为了社会层面更崇高的利益。

• 词意选选看 •

1. sentiment ____
2. conceal ____
3. propose ____
4. skeptical ____
5. speculate ____
6. boost ____
7. stake ____
8. process ____
9. sole ____
10. optimise ____

a. 提议
b. 情绪
c. 加工；处理
d. 唯一的
e. 股份
f. 掩盖
g. 怀疑的
h. 优化
i. 推测
j. 增加

• 拓展阅读 •

监控资本主义

Surveillance capitalism describes a market driven process where the commodity for sale is your personal data, and the capture and production of this data relies on mass surveillance of the internet. This activity is often carried out by companies that provide us with free online services, such as search engines and social media platforms. These companies collect and scrutinise our online behaviours (likes, dislikes, searches, social networks, purchases) to produce data that can be further used for commercial purposes. And it's often done without us understanding the full extent of the surveillance.

延伸思考：如何遏制监控资本主义？

第 2 天

Fake news is back in the real news. A study released this month found that the 100 most widely shared fake news stories of the year had received an estimated 158.9 million Facebook views between January and October. The European Union recently scolded social media giants, demanding they do more to combat fabricated content, and Mark Zuckerberg admitted that Facebook has caught bot-nets aimed at interfering in the 2020 U.S. elections.

But the most effective way to tackle the fake news onslaught isn't attempting to stamp out its sources. Instead, we need to focus on consumers. Deal with the demand, and the supply will become irrelevant. Educating the public is the key.

First, the bad news: Too many Americans don't have basic media literacy skills. The good news is that it's not hard to teach people to identify fake news. In our research, we've found even quick educational sessions can be effective. Targeting the reception of fake news can succeed where efforts to target production have failed or, at best, shown mixed results.

Social media companies have already been working to constrain the impact of fake news. Facebook has its election "war room" and has partnered with fact-checking services to minimize the prevalence of fake news content on the platform. But these efforts have been controversial, and a key issue of debate in the lead-up to the 2020 election. Obvious concerns arise when private companies police public discourse. Moreover, despite all these efforts, fake news remains widespread, polluting recent elections for the European Parliament, for example.

The problem with social media platforms goes far deeper than the content on them. The overall design of these platforms makes them hotbeds for misinformation, bias and fruitless bickering. To increase ad revenue, algorithms are weighted toward stories that get the most engagement. Often, those stories are inflammatory, misleading or outright false. Social media companies may show well-intentioned concern, but they will stop short of reforms that threaten their business models.

Therefore, it's up to users to approach the 21-century media environment, driven by news on social media, with more attention, care and skill. Students and adults need to learn how to research information online, determine the reliability of sources, understand bias, identify fake news, withstand emotional appeals, evaluate evidence and engage viewpoints different than their own.

Teaching these basic media literacy and critical thinking skills will not only help them resist fake news; it can also help stem the broader deterioration of public discourse, of which fake news is just one particularly alarming example.

文章大意

第一段：当前社交媒体中假新闻泛滥。

第二、三段：对抗假新闻最有效的办法是培养新闻读者的媒体素养，而非试图铲除假新闻本身。

第四、五段：社交媒体虽然已经着手应对假新闻问题，但其自身的特性以及利益局限性使其无法彻底地解决这一问题。

第六段：培养用户的媒体素养不仅能解决假新闻问题，还能遏制公共言论的进一步恶化。

逐段精讲

Para. 1 Fake news is back in the real news. A study released this month found that the 100 most widely shared fake news stories of the year had received an estimated 158.9 million Facebook views between January and October. The European Union recently scolded social media giants, demanding they do more to combat fabricated content, and Mark Zuckerberg admitted that Facebook has caught **bot-nets** aimed at interfering in the 2020 U.S. elections.

译文 假新闻问题又重新出现在真实的新闻中了。本月发布的一项研究表明，2019年最广为流传的100条假新闻1月至10月间在脸书上的总浏览量大约为1.589亿次。欧盟近日谴责了媒体巨头并要求它们采取更多行动来对抗不实信息，而马克·扎克伯格承认脸书已经查到了意在干涉2020年美国总统大选的僵尸网络。

背景知识

bot-net：僵尸网络，是指黑客利用自己编写的分布式拒绝服务攻击程序将数万个沦陷的机器，即黑客常说的傀儡机或"肉鸡"（肉机），组织成一个个命令与控制节点，用来发送垃圾数据包，使攻击目标瘫痪。通常蠕虫病毒也可以被利用来组成僵尸网络。

生词点睛

scold v. 斥责	fabricated adj. 捏造的
interfere v. 干涉；干预	election n. 选举

重点表达

❖ aimed at 意在……

Teachers have joined a strike **aimed at** forcing the government to pay overdue salaries and allowances. 教师加入了旨在迫使政府支付拖欠的薪水和津贴的罢工。

Para. 2 But the most effective way to tackle the fake news onslaught isn't attempting to stamp out its sources. Instead, we need to focus on consumers. Deal with the demand, and the supply will become irrelevant. Educating the public is the key.

译文 然而最有效的解决假新闻猖獗的方法并不是试图铲除其根源；相反，我们应该关注的是新闻用户们。只要处理好了需求问题，有无供给就无关紧要了。教育好大众是其中的关键。

生词点睛

onslaught n. 攻击；猛攻	irrelevant adj. 不相关的

重点表达

❖ stamp out sth. 根除；杜绝

The sanitary board tries to **stamp out** the epidemic. 卫生局试图消灭这种流行病。

Para. 3 First, the bad news: Too many Americans don't have basic media literacy skills. The good news is that it's not hard to teach people to identify fake news. In our research, we've found even quick educational sessions can be effective. Targeting the reception of fake news can succeed where efforts to target production have failed or, at best, shown mixed results.

译文 先说坏消息：太多的美国人不具备基本的媒体文字素养。好消息是教人们识别假新闻并不难。我们在研究中发现，甚至连短期教学都会起效。以假新闻的接收为目标，可以解决以产出为目标无法解决或只解决了一部分的问题。

生词点睛

| literacy n. 读写能力；识字 | session n. 会议；学年 |

重点表达

❖ mixed results 复杂的结果；喜忧参半的结果
The recent reform will bring about **mixed results**. 最近的改革将会带来喜忧参半的结果。

Para. 4 Social media companies have already been working to constrain the impact of fake news. Facebook has its election "war room" and has partnered with fact-checking services to minimize the prevalence of fake news content on the platform. But these efforts have been controversial, and a key issue of debate in the lead-up to the 2020 election. Obvious concerns arise when private companies police public discourse. Moreover, despite all these efforts, fake news remains widespread, polluting recent elections for the **European Parliament**, for example.

译文 社交媒体公司已经开始着手控制假新闻造成的影响。脸书成立了自己的大选"作战指挥室"并辅以核实服务，以尽可能地减少平台上假新闻的泛滥。但关于这些做法一直存在争议，这本身就是2020年大选前夕的一个重要议题。私企监督公众言论的行为引发了显著的担忧。此外，尽管已经做出了上述努力，假新闻仍然猖獗，还影响了欧洲议会最近的选举。

背景知识

European Parliament：欧洲议会，其前身是1952年成立的欧洲煤钢共同体议会，1962年改称"欧洲议会"，它是欧盟三大机构（欧盟理事会、欧盟委员会、欧洲议会）之一，为欧盟的立法、监督和咨询机构，总部设在法国城市斯特拉斯堡。

生词点睛

constrain v. 限制；约束	**war room** 作战指挥室
partner v. 与……搭档；协作	**prevalence** n. 流行；普遍
lead-up n. 先导；前奏	**discourse** n. 演讲；谈话

重点表达

❖ despite all these efforts... 尽管已做出了上述这些努力……

Despite all these efforts, many people have grown away from the classics of Chinese thought and literature. 尽管已经做出了上述种种努力，但许多人还是与中国传统思想和文化渐行渐远。

Para. 5　The problem with social media platforms goes far deeper than the content on them. The overall design of these platforms makes them hotbeds for misinformation, bias and fruitless bickering. To increase ad revenue, algorithms are weighted toward stories that get the most engagement. Often, those stories are inflammatory, misleading or outright false. Social media companies may show well-intentioned concern, but they will stop short of reforms that threaten their business models.

译文　社交媒体平台面临的问题远不止是内容层面的。这些平台的整体设计特点使它们成了虚假信息、偏见以及无意义的争吵的温床。出于增加广告收入的目的，算法会倾向于那些参与度高的新闻。一般来说，这类新闻要么有煽动性，要么有误导性，要么就是纯粹的假新闻。社交媒体公司或许展现出了一些善意的考量，但他们绝不会进行威胁到自己营利模式的改革。

生词点睛

hotbed *n.* 温床	**misinformation** *n.* 虚假信息
bicker *v.* 斗嘴；争吵	**inflammatory** *adj.* 煽动性的
misleading *adj.* 误导性的	**outright** *adv.* 完全彻底地

重点表达

❖ hotbeds for sth. 某事物的温床

Social networking sites have become lucrative **hotbeds for** cyber scams. 社交网络已经成为网络诈骗获利的温床。

❖ be weighted toward sth. 倾向于；有利于；使加权

Most "global" stock funds **are** heavily **weighted toward** stocks with the high values. 大多数全球型股票基金都重仓持有高估值的股票。

Para. 6 Therefore, it's up to users to approach the 21-century media environment, driven by news on social media, with more attention, care and skill. Students and adults need to learn how to research information online, determine the reliability of sources, understand bias, identify fake news, withstand emotional appeals, evaluate evidence and engage viewpoints different than their own. Teaching these basic media literacy and critical thinking skills will not only help them resist fake news; it can also help stem the broader deterioration of public discourse, of which fake news is just one particularly alarming example.

译文 因此，改善由社交媒体新闻主导的21世纪媒体环境的重任就落到了用户身上，用户需要对媒体新闻更加关注和关心，并具备更高的素质。学生和成年人需要学习如何研究网上的信息，判断信息源的可靠性，理解其中的偏见，识别假新闻，抵制情绪化的煽动，评估证据并试图理解与自身观点不同的意见。教会他们这些基本的媒体素养和批判性思考方法不仅能帮他们抵御假新闻，还能阻止公共言论的进一步恶化，假新闻只是其中一个特别具有警示作用的例子而已。

专题三 企业与社会

生词点睛

approach v. 着手处理；接近	reliability n. 可靠性
withstand v. 承受；抵制	stem v. 阻止
deterioration n. 恶化	

重点表达

❖ it is up to sb. to do sth. 做某事的责任在于某人；取决于某人去做某事

Railway lines are dangerous places and **it is up to** parents **to** inform their children of the dangers. 铁路是危险的地方，父母有责任告知孩子们其中的危险。

It is up to you **to** decide whether to go or stay. 由你来决定是走是留。

词意选选看

1. interfere _____
2. election _____
3. onslaught _____
4. irrelevant _____
5. literacy _____
6. constrain _____
7. prevalence _____
8. misinformation _____
9. misleading _____
10. withstand _____

a. 不相关的
b. 识字能力
c. 承受；抵制
d. 大选
e. 虚假信息
f. 干预
g. 约束
h. 攻击；猛攻
i. 流行
j. 误导性的

拓展阅读

媒体素养教育

　　Media literacy education provides tools to help people critically analyze messages, offers opportunities for learners to broaden their experience of media, and helps them develop creative skills in making their own media messages. Critical analyses can include identifying author, purpose and point of view, examining construction techniques and genres, examining patterns of media representation, and detecting propaganda, censorship, and bias in news and public affairs programming (and the reasons for these). Media literacy education may explore how structural features—such as media ownership, or its funding model—affect the information presented.

延伸思考：媒体素养教育在信息时代具有哪些独特的意义？

第 3 天

Through non-compete clauses, employers have robbed tens of millions of workers of the right to practice their trade where they want. Non-competes can bar workers from accepting new employment in their field or industry for a year or more after they leave. Policymakers are now engaged in an unacknowledged debate over how to regulate non-competes. Should all workers have the freedom to find and take new work when and where they want, or should this right be conditional on income or occupation?

A universal national solution is necessary. The freedom to exit should be a basic right, not a privilege for a certain group of workers. Even if Congress does not pass the Workforce Mobility Act, the next president, acting through the Federal Trade Commission (FTC), can ban non-competes and restore all workers' freedom. Nineteen state attorneys general endorsed FTC action as "offering the quickest, most comprehensive regulatory path to protecting all workers from these exploitative contracts."

Somewhere between 36 million and 60 million workers are bound by non-compete clauses today. Hardly any profession is free from them. Employers generally don't enforce non-compete restrictions in court—and don't need to. Simply imposing a non-compete discourages workers from looking for new work and switching jobs. Even for well-paid professionals with access to legal services, the mere threat of employer enforcement is often enough to bind them to their current jobs.

Importantly, many employers ask job applicants whether they are bound by a non-compete and use the existence of a non-compete as a screen when reviewing applications. For employers, why run even a slight risk of litigation with a new hire's former employer when job seekers are plentiful?

In a fair labor market, firms afraid of losing workers have a simple way of retaining them: raise salaries, improve benefits, and offer promotions. They can also use employment contracts that commit both parties to the employment relationship for a fixed period.

Employers in a wide range of industries have deprived workers of the basic freedom to leave their jobs to pursue their trades elsewhere. In an economy with low union density and persistent unemployment or underemployment, threatening to leave is often the only way millions of workers can obtain decent wages or fair treatment. But for workers subject to a non-compete, speaking up about pay or other conditions of employment can mean not only losing their current job, but also risking their entire livelihood. The freedom to leave should be universal, not available only to some.

文章大意

第一段：决策者当前正在商讨是否要对竞业禁止条款进行限制与监管。

第二段：应该出台一个全国性的政策以保证所有人的离职和求职自由。

第三段：当前受竞业禁止条款约束的人数众多，企业仅仅靠与员工签订竞业禁止条款就能有效限制员工的离职。

第四段：在劳动力充足的情况下，企业没必要承担不必要的法律风险，故竞业禁止条款已成为企业筛选求职者的手段之一。

第五段：企业完全可以通过升职加薪或签订劳动合同的方式留住员工。

第六段：离职和换工作是广大员工争取应得利益的核心手段，每个人都应享有离职自由。

逐段精讲

Para. 1 Through non-compete clauses, employers have robbed tens of millions of workers of the right to practice their trade where they want. Non-competes can bar workers from accepting new employment in their field or industry for a year or more after they leave. Policymakers are now engaged in an unacknowledged debate over how to regulate non-competes. Should all workers have the freedom to find and take new work when and where they want, or should this right be conditional on income or occupation?

译文 通过竞业禁止条款，企业已经夺走了上千万员工自由择业的权利。竞业禁止条款可以在员工离职后的一年甚至更长的一段时间里禁止员工接受同领域或同行业的新工作。决策者们目前正在进行关于如何监管竞业禁止条款的非公开讨论。所有员工是否都理应自由地寻找并接受自己中意的工作，抑或拥有这种权利是否应该取决于他们的收入和职业？

专题三　企业与社会

生词点睛

clause *n.* 条款；从句	**rob** *v.* 抢劫；掠夺
unacknowledged *adj.* 非正式的；非公开的	**regulate** *v.* 监管
conditional *adj.* 有条件的	**occupation** *n.* 工作；职业

重点表达

❖ be conditional on sth. 取决于某事物；以某事物为条件
Their success **is conditional on** their efforts. 能否成功取决于他们的努力。

Para. 2　A universal national solution is necessary. The freedom to exit should be a basic right, not a privilege for a certain group of workers. Even if Congress does not pass the Workforce Mobility Act, the next president, acting through the **Federal Trade Commission (FTC)**, can ban non-competes and restore all workers' freedom. Nineteen state attorneys general endorsed FTC action as "offering the quickest, most comprehensive regulatory path to protecting all workers from these exploitative contracts."

译文　出台一个全国性的解决方案是很有必要的。离职的自由本应是一种基本权利，而非只属于某些人的特权。即便国会没有通过《劳动力流动性法案》，下届总统也能通过美国联邦贸易委员会来取缔竞业禁止条款并恢复员工们的自由。十九个州的司法部部长都支持美国联邦贸易委员会所采取的行动，因为这是"保护员工免受合同压榨的最快速、最全面的监管措施"。

背景知识

Federal Trade Commission (FTC)：美国联邦贸易委员会，是执行多种反托拉斯和保护消费者法律的联邦机构。美国联邦贸易委员会成立于1914年，目的是确保国家市场行为具有竞争性，且繁荣、高效地发展，不受不合理的约束。美国联邦贸易委员会也通过消除不合理的和欺骗性的条例或规章来确保和促进市场运营的顺畅。

生词点睛

universal *adj.* 普遍的；共同的	**privilege** *n.* 特权
Congress *n.* 国会	**mobility** *n.* 流动性
attorney *n.* 律师	**endorse** *v.* 赞同；支持
comprehensive *adj.* 综合的；全面的	**exploitative** *adj.* 剥削性的

重点表达

❖ path to sth. 通往……之路

He promised that within 100 days he would put the country on the **path to** economic recovery.
他许诺在100天内让国家走上经济复兴之路。

Para. 3 Somewhere between 36 million and 60 million workers are bound by non-compete clauses today. Hardly any profession is free from them. Employers generally don't enforce non-compete restrictions in court—and don't need to. Simply imposing a non-compete discourages workers from looking for new work and switching jobs. Even for well-paid professionals with access to legal services, the mere threat of employer enforcement is often enough to bind them to their current jobs.

译文 如今受竞业禁止条款限制的员工总数在3 600万至6 000万人之间。几乎没有任何职业能幸免。企业基本不会在法庭上执行竞业禁止条款，因为他们根本不需要这样做。仅仅是签署竞业禁止条款就能起到阻止员工找工作和换工作的作用。即便对于那些能获得法律服务的高收入人士而言，雇主光是威胁要执行条款往往就足以把他们束缚在当前的工作岗位上。

生词点睛

enforce *v.* 执行；行使	**discourage** *v.* 阻拦；阻止
switch *v.* 切换	**mere** *adj.* 唯一的
bind *v.* 捆绑；系；结合	

重点表达

❖ somewhere between A and B 介于 A 与 B 之间的数量/状态

The Queen is believed to earn **somewhere between** seven million **and** one hundred million pounds. 据说女王的收入大约在 700 万至 1 亿英镑之间。

❖ be bound by 受……的约束

If her patient threatens to kill someone, she **is bound by** law to inform the police. 如果她的病人威胁要杀人，那么根据法律她有责任通知警察。

Para. 4 Importantly, many employers ask job applicants whether they are bound by a non-compete and use the existence of a non-compete as a screen when reviewing applications. For employers, why run even a slight risk of litigation with a new hire's former employer when job seekers are plentiful?

译文 重要的是，很多企业会询问求职者是否受竞业禁止条款的约束，并将其作为一种筛选求职者的手段。对企业而言，在求职者充裕的情况下，何必承担与新员工的前任雇主打官司的哪怕一点点的风险呢？

生词点睛

applicant n. 申请人	screen n. 筛选
slight adj. 轻微的	litigation n. 打官司；诉讼

重点表达

❖ run a risk of sth. 冒着……的风险

If you keep working in such a temperature, you will **run a risk of** getting heat stroke. 如果在这样的温度下继续工作，你就会有中暑的危险。

Para. 5 In a fair labor market, firms afraid of losing workers have a simple way of retaining them: raise salaries, improve benefits, and offer promotions. They can also use employment contracts

译文 在一个公平的劳动力市场中，害怕失去员工的企业有一个简单的办法留住他们：增加薪水、改善福利待遇、提供晋升机会。企业也可以

121

that commit both parties to the employment relationship for a fixed period.

通过就业合同使双方在特定时期内保持雇佣关系。

生词点睛

| **retain** *v.* 保留 | **promotion** *n.* 晋升 |

Para. 6 Employers in a wide range of industries have deprived workers of the basic freedom to leave their jobs to pursue their trades elsewhere. In an economy with low union density and persistent unemployment or underemployment, threatening to leave is often the only way millions of workers can obtain decent wages or fair treatment. But for workers subject to a non-compete, speaking up about pay or other conditions of employment can mean not only losing their current job, but also risking their entire livelihood. The freedom to leave should be universal, not available only to some.

译文 各行各业的雇主都剥夺了员工离职并另谋高就的基本权利。在一个工会密度低、失业或就业不充分问题长期存在的经济体中，威胁离职往往是上千万员工们争取合理薪资或公平待遇的唯一手段。但对于受竞业禁止条款限制的员工而言，提及薪水或其他工作情况可能不仅会使他们失去现有的工作，还会将他们的整个生计置于危险之中。人人都应该享有离职的自由，而不仅限于某些人。

生词点睛

| **pursue** *v.* 追求 | **density** *n.* 密度 |
| **persistent** *adj.* 持续的 | **decent** *adj.* 体面的；适当的 |

重点表达

❖ deprive A of B 剥夺 A 的 B

If you **deprive** them **of** education, the nation cannot progress. 如果剥夺了他们受教育的权利，国家就无法进步。

❖ be subject to sth. 服从于……；受……支配

This proposal **is subject to** your approval. 这项议案需要得到你的审批。

词意选选看

1. regulate ____
2. conditional ____
3. occupation ____
4. universal ____
5. privilege ____
6. endorse ____
7. discourage ____
8. switch ____
9. bind ____
10. pursue ____

a. 职业
b. 特权
c. 监管
d. 支持
e. 切换
f. 普遍的
g. 捆绑
h. 有条件的
i. 追求
j. 阻拦

拓展阅读

竞业禁止条款

The use of non-compete clauses is premised on the possibility that upon their termination or resignation, an employee might begin working for a competitor or start a business, and gain competitive advantage by exploiting confidential information about their former employer's operations or trade secrets, or sensitive information such as customer/client lists, business practices, upcoming products, and marketing plans.

延伸思考：如何理解竞业禁止条款存在的合理性？

第 4 天

    The 2010s will be remembered for a new era in the development of capitalism. Apple, Amazon and Microsoft are closing the decade as the world's first trillion-dollar companies. Last year, Apple's revenue was larger than Vietnam's GDP, while Amazon's research and development spending alone is almost as much as Iceland's GDP. Facebook boasts 2.4 billion users, a population larger than that of every continent except Asia.

    Big tech may offer much to us as consumers but, as the decade progressed, it became clear that it presents a problem for us as citizens who want elections that adhere to advertising laws and are free from foreign interference. It's also a problem for people who want to live in towns with functioning retail high streets, and where logistics and delivery are secure, proper jobs, not rendered precarious by Amazon's ruthless margin-squeezing.

    Companies this size are even bad for capitalism itself. They dominate markets and suppress competition: Google and Facebook control an estimated 60% of all online advertising, and, in the US, Amazon gets four in every 10 dollars spent online. Should another tech company show promise, one of these firms just gobbles it up.

    Big tech moved at a scale and speed that states and regulators couldn't match. As marketplaces, they benefit from "network effects", where each additional user improves the utility of a service, producing a positive feedback loop of growth. Running costs barely change as more people join. This has allowed their rise to surpass those of other boom industries in the past, from automobiles to oil: one additional car on the roads, for instance, causes more congestion.

    In the US and UK, with rightwing populists in power, greater state regulation may not go exactly as tech commentators of the early 2010s hoped. There are fundamental tensions in what we are asking of Facebook, Google and Twitter. We fear how far they shape and control the information billions see—but, in seeking action on abusive content and misinformation, we ask that they exert yet more control, not less.

    The social media era has already gone: we're shifting away from public press towards private and small group messaging. I expect to see tech companies getting better with regulations that discourage hostile digital behaviour—though I hold little hope for decisive action on the big issues of antitrust. The tech headlines of 2019—"Facebook revenues soar despite $5.1bn in fines",

"Google hit with 'historic' monopoly abuse investigation"—may well predict the state of things in 2029.

文章大意

第一段：21世纪的第二个十年，科技巨头的大幅发展将资本主义带入全新阶段。

第二、三段：科技巨头的发展在为消费者带来便利的同时，也给公民和社会带来了问题。超大体量的科技巨头甚至对资本主义市场的竞争与繁荣都是有害的。

第四段：与汽车等传统行业不同，科技巨头一方面得益于网络效应，一方面又不会因为用户数量的增长而承担更多的运营成本，这使它们达到了前所未有的发展程度。

第五段：当前社会对科技巨头提出的多方面要求中存在根本性的矛盾。

第六段：政府不太可能在反垄断问题上采取果断措施，2019年科技巨头的垄断现状或在十年后也不会有所改变。

逐段精讲

Para. 1 The 2010s will be remembered for a new era in the development of capitalism. Apple, Amazon and Microsoft are closing the decade as the world's first trillion-dollar companies. Last year, Apple's revenue was larger than Vietnam's GDP, while Amazon's research and development spending alone is almost as much as Iceland's GDP. Facebook boasts 2.4 billion users, a population larger than that of every continent except Asia.

译文 21世纪的第二个十年将会因为资本主义进入全新的发展阶段而被后人铭记。作为世界上第一批市值达万亿的公司，苹果、亚马逊和微软正在为这个时代画上句号。去年，苹果公司的营收已经超过了越南的GDP，而亚马逊光是一项研发支出就几乎可以比肩冰岛的GDP了。脸书自诩拥有24亿用户，比除亚洲外的任何一个大洲的人口总数都要多。

生词点睛

era *n.* 时代	**trillion** *n.* 万亿；兆
boast *v.* 自夸；吹嘘	**continent** *n.* 大陆

Para. 2　Big tech may offer much to us as consumers but, as the decade progressed, it became clear that it presents a problem for us as citizens who want elections that adhere to advertising laws and are free from foreign interference. It's also a problem for people who want to live in towns with functioning retail high streets, and where logistics and delivery are secure, not rendered precarious by Amazon's ruthless margin-squeezing.

译文　科技巨头或许能为身为消费者的我们提供很多东西，但随着这十年时间的推移而越发清晰的是，科技巨头对身为公民，希望选举遵守广告法且不受境外势力影响的我们而言是个问题。对于那些希望生活在拥有正常的商业街的城市里的人而言，科技巨头同样是个问题，在那些城市中，物流和快递是安全的，不会因为亚马逊无底线地缩减成本的行为而岌岌可危。

生词点睛

high street 大街；主要商业街道	**logistics** *n.* 物流
render *v.* 使成为；使变得	**ruthless** *adj.* 残酷无情的

重点表达

❖ adhere to sth. 遵守……

We must **adhere to** the principle of making study serve the practical purpose. 我们必须坚持学以致用的原则。

❖ be free from 不受……的影响

This town **is free from** air pollution. 这座城市没有空气污染。

Para. 3　Companies this size are even bad for capitalism itself. They dominate markets and

译文　如此大体量的企业甚至对资本主义自身都是有害的。它们支配着市场

suppress competition: Google and Facebook control an estimated 60% of all online advertising, and, in the US, Amazon gets four in every 10 dollars spent online. Should another tech company show promise, one of these firms just gobbles it up.

并压制了竞争行为：谷歌和脸书控制了大约 60% 的线上广告；而在美国，每 10 美元的线上消费中，就有 4 美元进了亚马逊的账户。一旦有其他科技企业展现出良好的发展前景，上述的某个巨头便会直接将其吞并。

生词点睛

| **suppress** *v.* 压制；阻止 | **promise** *n.* 前途；许诺 |

重点表达

❖ gobble up sth. 狼吞虎咽；吞并
The children **gobble up** their food and rushed out to play. 孩子们狼吞虎咽地吃完饭就冲出去玩了。

Para. 4 Big tech moved at a scale and speed that states and regulators couldn't match. As marketplaces, they benefit from "**network effects**", where each additional user improves the utility of a service, producing a positive feedback loop of growth. Running costs barely change as more people join. This has allowed their rise to surpass those of other boom industries in the past, from automobiles to oil: one additional car on the roads, for instance, causes more congestion.

译文 科技巨头以各州政府和监管者无法企及的规模和速度发展着。作为交易市场，这些企业受益于"网络效应"，每一个新用户都会增加其服务的效用，进而形成公司发展的正反馈循环。其运营成本几乎不会因为新用户的加入而改变。这使得科技巨头的崛起更甚于汽车和石油等过去繁荣一时的行业：因为就汽车行业而言，路上每增加一辆汽车，便会造成更严重的拥堵。

背景知识

network effects： 网络效应，是指产品价值随购买这种产品及其兼容产品的消费者的数量增加而增加。例如，在电信系统中，当人们都不使用电话时，安装电话是没有价值的，而电话越普及，安装电话的价值就越高。在互联网、传媒、航空运输、金融等行业中普遍存在网络效应。

生词点睛

scale *n.* 规模	**regulator** *n.* 监管者
loop *n.* 循环	**surpass** *v.* 超过
boom *n.* 繁荣；激增	**congestion** *n.* 拥堵

Para. 5 In the US and UK, with rightwing populists in power, greater state regulation may not go exactly as tech commentators of the early 2010s hoped. There are fundamental tensions in what we are asking of Facebook, Google and Twitter. We fear how far they shape and control the information billions see—but, in seeking action on abusive content and misinformation, we ask that they exert yet more control, not less.

译文 随着美国和英国右翼民粹主义人士掌权，更有力的国家监管措施并不完全像 21 世纪第二个十年早期科技评论员们所期盼的那样。我们当前对脸书、谷歌和推特提出的要求中存在根本性的矛盾。我们一方面害怕它们对数十亿人民所接触的信息的影响力和控制力过强，但另一方面，在治理恶意内容和虚假信息时，我们又要求它们施加更多而非更少的管控。

生词点睛

populist *n.* 民粹主义者	**commentator** *n.* 评论员
tension *n.* 矛盾；紧张关系	**abusive** *adj.* 恶意的；辱骂的

Para. 6 The social media era has already gone: we're shifting away from public press towards private and small group messaging. I expect to see tech companies getting better with regulations that discourage hostile digital behaviour—though I hold little hope for decisive action on the big issues of antitrust. The tech headlines of 2019—"Facebook revenues soar despite $5.1bn in fines", "Google hit

译文 社交媒体时代已然终结：我们正从公众出版转向私人化、小群体化的信息发送模式。我相信阻止恶意数字行为的监管措施会让科技公司越来越好，虽然在反垄断这样的重大问题上，我不指望政府会采取任何果断的行动。"被罚 51 亿美元，脸书的收入仍然飙升"以及"谷歌遭遇'历史上'滥用垄断地

with 'historic' monopoly abuse investigation"—may well predict the state of things in 2029.

位调查"这些 2019 年度科技板块的头条很可能到了 2029 年仍不过时。

生词点睛

| **hostile** *adj.* 恶意的；敌意的 | **decisive** *adj.* 果断的 |
| **antitrust** *n.* 反垄断；反托拉斯 | **soar** *v.* 飙升 |

重点表达

❖ shift away from A towards B 从 A 转向 B

Slowly, the focus of public attention began to **shift away from** knowing what such people did **towards** knowing what they looked like. 公众的注意力逐渐由了解这些人做了什么转移到他们长什么样子。

词意选选看

1. era ____
2. render ____
3. ruthless ____
4. suppress ____
5. promise ____
6. scale ____
7. surpass ____
8. boom ____
9. tension ____
10. soar ____

a. 压制
b. 残酷无情的
c. 前途
d. 时代
e. 紧张关系
f. 使变得
g. 规模
h. 飙升
i. 超过
j. 繁荣

拓展阅读

网络效应

Network effects become significant after a certain subscription percentage has been achieved, called critical mass. At the critical mass point, the value obtained from the good or service is greater than or equal to the price paid for the good or service. As the value of the good is determined by the user base, this implies that after a certain number of people have subscribed to the service or purchased the good, additional people will subscribe to the service or purchase the good due to the value exceeding the price.

延伸思考：网络效应带来的收益是否存在极限？

第 5 天

It hurts to keep secrets. Secrecy is associated with lower well-being, worse health, and less satisfying relationships. Research has linked secrecy to increased anxiety, depression, symptoms of poor health, and even the more rapid progression of disease. There is a seemingly obvious explanation for these harms: Hiding secrets is hard work. You have to watch what you say. If asked about something related to the secret, you must be careful not to slip up. This could require evasion or even deception. Constant vigilance and concealment can be exhausting.

New research, however, suggests that the harm of secrets doesn't really come from the hiding after all. The real problem with keeping a secret is not that you have to hide it, but that you have to live with it, and think about it. To better understand the harms of secrecy, my colleagues and I first set out to understand what secrets people keep, and how often they keep them. We found that 97% of people have at least one secret at any given moment, and people have, on average, 13 secrets.

Across several studies, we asked participants to estimate how frequently they concealed their secret during conversations with others, and also how frequently they thought about the secret outside of social interactions. We found that the more frequently people simply thought about their secrets, the lower their well-being.

Following up this research, a new paper reveals why thinking about secrets is so harmful. Turning the question around, we examined the consequences of confiding secrets. We found that when a person confides a secret to a third party, it does not reduce how often they have to conceal the secret from others who are still kept in the dark. Rather, it reduces how often their mind wanders toward the secret in irrelevant moments.

The act of confiding a secret can feel cathartic and relieving. But mere catharsis is not enough. When confiding a secret, what is actually helpful is the conversation that follows. People report that when sharing a secret with another person, they often receive emotional support, useful guidance, and helpful advice. These forms of support make people feel more confident and capable in coping with the secret. When people find a healthier way of thinking about their secret, they ruminate less on it, and have improved well-being.

This new science of secrecy brings both good and bad news. The bad news is that even when we are not hiding our secrets, they are still very much with us, and can still hurt us. The good news is that even when we choose to still keep something secret, talking to another person can make the world of difference.

文章大意

第一段：指出保守秘密会给人带来伤害。
第二段：指出保密有危害的真正原因。
第三段：研究表明思考秘密的频率越高，害处越大。
第四段：从反面论证思考秘密是有害的。
第五段：指出吐露秘密的好处。
第六段：指出保密的好处和坏处。

逐段精讲

Para. 1 It hurts to keep secrets. Secrecy is associated with lower well-being, worse health, and less satisfying relationships. Research has linked secrecy to increased anxiety, depression, symptoms of poor health, and even the more rapid progression of disease. There is a seemingly obvious explanation for these harms: Hiding secrets is hard work. You have to watch what you say. If asked about something related to the secret, you must be careful not to slip up. This could require evasion or even deception. Constant vigilance and concealment can be exhausting.

译文 保守秘密很痛苦。保密与幸福感较低、健康状况较差以及人际关系不太令人满意相关。研究将保密与焦虑、抑郁、不健康症状的增加，甚至病情的快速恶化联系了起来。对这些危害有一个看似明显的解释：隐藏秘密是一项艰苦的工作。你得时刻注意你所说的话。如果被问及与这个秘密有关的事情，你必须得小心，不要泄密。这可能就需要你采取逃避甚至是欺骗的方式。经常保持警惕和隐瞒秘密会令人筋疲力尽。

专题三 企业与社会

生词点睛

anxiety *n.* 焦虑，不安，担心	**depression** *n.* 抑郁症
evasion *n.* 逃避；回避	**slip up** 出差错，疏忽
deception *n.* 欺骗；蒙骗	**vigilance** *n.* 警惕，警戒
exhausting *adj.* 使人筋疲力尽的	

重点表达

❖ link A to B 将 A 和 B 连接或联系起来

The new bridge will **link** the island **to** the mainland. 新的桥梁将把该岛与大陆连接在一起。

Para. 2 New research, however, suggests that the harm of secrets doesn't really come from the hiding after all. The real problem with keeping a secret is not that you have to hide it, but that you have to live with it, and think about it. To better understand the harms of secrecy, my colleagues and I first set out to understand what secrets people keep, and how often they keep them. We found that 97% of people have at least one secret at any given moment, and people have, on average, 13 secrets.

译文 然而，新的研究表明，秘密的危害并非真正来自隐藏秘密。保守秘密的真正问题不是你必须隐藏它，而是你必须忍受并思考它。为了更好地理解保密的危害，我和我的同事们首先着手了解人们保守什么秘密，以及他们保守秘密的频率。我们发现 97% 的人在任何特定时刻都至少有一个秘密，平均每人有 13 个秘密。

生词点睛

colleague *n.* 同事，同僚	**at any given moment** 在任何特定时刻
on average 平均来看	

重点表达

❖ be not that..., but that... 不是……，而是……

The great tragedy of life **is not that** men perish, **but that** they cease to love. 人生的巨大悲剧不是人们死亡，而是他们不再去爱。

❖ live with 忍受，容忍

Many politicians find such laws difficult to **live with**. 许多政治家认为难以容忍这样的法律。

❖ to better understand... 为了更好地理解……

To better understand it, you can actually use a visual analogy. 为了更好地理解这种情况，你可以利用视觉类比。

Para. 3 Across several studies, we asked participants to estimate how frequently they concealed their secret during conversations with others, and also how frequently they thought about the secret outside of social interactions. We found that the more frequently people simply thought about their secrets, the lower their well-being.

译文 在几项研究中，我们要求参与者估算一下他们在与他人交谈时隐瞒秘密的频率，以及他们在社交互动之外思考秘密的频率。我们发现，人们思考自己秘密的频率越高，他们的幸福感就越低。

生词点睛

estimate v. 估计，估算	frequently adv. 经常地，频繁地
social interaction 社交互动	

重点表达

❖ We found that the + 比较级 ..., the + 比较级 ... 我们发现，越……，越……

We found that the more sophisticated the exposure assessment, **the less likely** it was that an effect would be reported. 我们发现暴露评估越复杂，报告健康影响的可能性就越小。

We found that the more we learn, **the more** we feel the need to learn. 我们发现越学越想学。

Para. 4 Following up this research, a new paper reveals why thinking about secrets is so harmful. Turning the question around, we examined the consequences of confiding secrets. We found that when a person confides a secret to a third party, it

译文 在这项研究之后，一篇新论文揭示了为什么思考秘密如此有害。换个角度来看这个问题，我们研究了吐露秘密的后果。我们发现，当一个人向第三方吐露秘密时，他们向那些

does not reduce how often they have to conceal the secret from others who are still kept in the dark. Rather, it reduces how often their mind wanders toward the secret in irrelevant moments.

对秘密一无所知的人隐瞒秘密的频率并不会降低。相反，降低的是他们在无关紧要时思考秘密的频率。

生词点睛

consequence *n.* 结果；后果	**confide** *v.* 吐露（隐私、秘密等）
wander *v.* 徘徊，闲逛	

重点表达

❖ turn the question around 换个角度来看这个问题

If we **turn the question around** and now say, what does the laughter sound like? 如果我们换个角度来看问题，现在说，笑声听起来是什么样子的？

❖ keep sb. in the dark 使……蒙在鼓里；对……保密

He's **keeping** me **in the dark** for some reason. 出于某种原因，他什么事都不告诉我。

Para. 5 The act of confiding a secret can feel cathartic and relieving. But mere catharsis is not enough. When confiding a secret, what is actually helpful is the conversation that follows. People report that when sharing a secret with another person, they often receive emotional support, useful guidance, and helpful advice. These forms of support make people feel more confident and capable in coping with the secret. When people find a healthier way of thinking about their secret, they ruminate less on it, and have improved well-being.

译文 吐露秘密的行为可以让人心旷神怡。但纯粹的宣泄是不够的。在吐露秘密时，真正有用的是人们之后的对话。人们说在与他人分享秘密时，他们往往会得到情感支持、实用的指导和有益的建议。这些形式的支持使人们更加自信同时更有能力应对这一秘密。当人们找到更健康的方式来思考他们的秘密时，便不会总是想起它，从而可以提高自己的幸福感。

生词点睛

cathartic *adj.* 精神宣泄的	**relieving** *adj.* 慰藉的；减轻的；缓和的
catharsis *n.* 精神发泄	**ruminate** *v.* 仔细思考，沉思

重点表达

❖ feel confident in doing sth. 对做某事有信心
We hope you have enjoyed learning with her and **feel more confident in** using English at work!
我们希望你们喜欢跟她一起学习，并能自信地使用职场英语！

Para. 6 This new science of secrecy brings both good and bad news. The bad news is that even when we are not hiding our secrets, they are still very much with us, and can still hurt us. The good news is that even when we choose to still keep something secret, talking to another person can make the world of difference.

译文 这种新的保密科学带来的既有好消息也有坏消息。坏消息是，即使我们没有隐瞒自己的秘密，那些秘密也仍然伴随着我们，仍然可以伤害我们。好消息是，即使我们选择继续保守一些秘密，与他人交谈依然会让世界变得不同。

重点表达

❖ be with sb. 在某人一边；和某人（观点）一致
I **am with** you there. 在那点上我同你意见一致。
The people **are with** him. 人民拥护他。

• 词意选选看 •

1. deception ____   a. 使人筋疲力尽的
2. slip up ____   b. 警惕
3. vigilance ____   c. 吐露（隐私、秘密等）
4. exhausting ____   d. 欺骗；蒙骗
5. confide ____   e. 出差错；疏忽

6. relieving _____   f. 仔细思考，沉思
7. consequence _____   g. 应对，处理
8. cathartic _____   h. 慰藉的；减轻的
9. cope with _____   i. 精神宣泄的
10. ruminate _____   j. 结果；后果

·拓展阅读·

关于保守或泄露秘密的研究结果

  Studies confirmed a hypothesized longitudinal contribution of keeping a secret all to oneself to psychosocial problems, including depressive mood, low self-concept clarity, low self-control, loneliness, and poor relationship quality. Furthermore, confiding versus continuing to keep a secret all to oneself was associated with decreased psychosocial problems after six months, whereas starting to keep a secret versus not doing so was associated with increased psychosocial problems. These results suggest that the keeping or confiding of secrets may affect adolescents' psychosocial well-being and adjustment.

延伸思考：保守秘密的意义何在？

专题四 政策与民生

导　言

　　翻开当今任何一份主流报刊，占据大部分版面的往往是与政府政策相关的话题。由于政策与民生类话题牵涉读者的切身利益，所以此类话题最受读者关注，也最受报刊评论员与考研命题人的青睐。

　　现代社会中，除了专题三提到的有关企业与市场监管的责任外，政府主要承担经济调节、科教文卫、社会服务这三方面的职能。首先，经济调节职能直接关系到人民的钱袋子问题。历年考研英语阅读真题中考查过有关就业市场、失业保险的话题。另外值得一提的是，在解决经济问题时，政府往往还需借助法律工具与财政工具，各位考生需要具有这两个领域的基本常识。

　　其次，在为高等院校选拔人才的研究生考试中，科教文卫职能中的科学与教育政策存在感极强：考研英语阅读真题中曾多次考查与学生有关的政策话题，而英语一在此基础上尤其偏爱反思高等教育路线的文章；此外，文体类政策话题也均有考查历史，如2020年英语一真题中关于"英国'文化城'"的文章，以及2017年英语二真题中关于"英国体育运动政策"的文章。

　　除了上述问题外，政府还需要尽可能地满足人民群众为实现幸福美好生活而提出的各类需求，这就是政府的社会服务职能。考研英语阅读中涉及较多的话题为公务员问题、移民问题、两性平等问题、住房与城市规划问题等。如果考生想要驾驭以上话题，就必须对相关问题的历史背景、政府的解决思路以及社会对此的主流评价有一定的了解。

　　上述三类职能以及相关话题构成了考研英语阅读中政策与民生类文章的选题区间，希望各位考生在学习本专题文章之余，还能积极关注日常生活中的各类时政要闻，建立起对当代大国政府的治理思路以及运行机制的全面认知，以满足考研的要求。

2010—2021年相关考研英语阅读真题

英语一

2012　Text-4　公务员系统中的工会

2014　Text-1　奥斯本的失业补贴新政

2016　Text-1　法国时尚行业新规

2017　Text-1　机场安检问题

2017　Text-3　GDP与幸福指数

2019	Text-4	网购税收规则的更改
2020	Text-1	英国"文化城"
2021	Text-2	扶贫项目与环境保护的关系

英语二

2010	Text-4	陪审团制度进化史
2011	Text-4	欧元区危机
2012	Text-1	作业政策反思
2013	Text-2	美国现行移民政策
2013	Text-4	企业高管中的女性配额政策
2014	Text-4	英国住房问题
2015	Text-2	"学一代"政策反思
2015	Text-4	美国就业形势和奥巴马医改
2017	Text-1	英国体育运动政策
2019	Text-3	美国农业外来劳动力问题
2021	Text-1	疫情下的"再培训"
2021	Text-2	英国脱欧后的粮食安全问题

第1天

A decade ago a ride-hailing service called UberCab launched in Silicon Valley. The business model relies on shareholders to subsidise cheap rides so that the company can squeeze out rivals and establish a monopoly. Uber's success is that 90 million people now use it in 700 cities around the world. After it floated on the stock market, its two founders became billionaires. While the owners of Uber have become immensely wealthy, the people who drive its cars have paid a heavy price. Unions say that Uber drivers in the UK earn an average of £5 an hour, well below the legal minimum wage of £8.21 for employees aged over 25.

Across Britain, gig work—part of a casualised, precarious and on-call jobs market—is growing at a giddy rate. The sector has more than doubled in size since 2016 and now accounts for 4.7 million workers. In part this is due to new technology: people are using apps on their mobile phones to sell their labour. Uncertain work is becoming the norm, with the result that unemployment statistics look better than the way Britons feel.

At present there are three categories of employment status in the UK: employee, worker and the self-employed. Only the first category is entitled to full employment rights, including redundancy payments, parental leave, and protection against unfair dismissal. The second category ought to have their minimum wage and trade union rights protected, as well as paid holiday entitlement. However, gig-economy firms assume their workers to be self-employed, and fight trade unions such as the Independent Workers' Union of Great Britain (IWGB) who claim otherwise. In almost every case workers in the gig economy have proved that they are in fact employees. It is absurd that judges must protect workers from forced self-employment.

It ought to be possible for workers to have flexible work without denying them basic rights. Businesses can only compete fairly if employment rules are equally applied and consistently enforced. On a deeper level, the gig economy is erasing what was for many the traditional goal of working: to buy free time. Instead we are being seduced and coerced into thinking that it is good to commercialise our leisure time and possessions. Unless we can turn away from such thinking, we shall see ourselves acting less like humans and more like companies.

文章大意

第一段：优步公司是通过压榨员工来发展壮大的。

第二段：英国的零工工作者正在快速增加，越来越多的人正通过APP出卖自己的劳动力。

第三段：相关企业不承认零工工作者的雇员身份，这使他们的权利缺乏应有的保障。

第四段：零工经济诱导人们将自己的闲暇时间视作一种经济资源并进行出售，这从根本上背离了人们通过工作换取自由的初衷。

逐段精讲

Para. 1 A decade ago a ride-hailing service called UberCab launched in Silicon Valley. The business model relies on shareholders to subsidise cheap rides so that the company can squeeze out rivals and establish a monopoly. **Uber**'s success is that 90 million people now use it in 700 cities around the world. After it floated on the stock market, its two founders became billionaires. While the owners of Uber have become immensely wealthy, the people who drive its cars have paid a heavy price. Unions say that Uber drivers in the UK earn an average of £5 an hour, well below the legal minimum wage of £8.21 for employees aged over 25.

译文 十年前，一个叫优步出租的叫车服务在硅谷上线了。其商业模式是依靠股东来补贴廉价出租服务，以此打压竞争对手并建立垄断地位。如今优步已在全世界700个城市成功获得了9 000万用户。在优步上市后，它的两位创始人成为亿万富翁。在老板们暴富的同时，为优步开车的司机们则付出了沉重的代价。各工会表示，英国优步司机的平均时薪为5英镑，远低于25岁以上工作者的法定最低工资标准（8.21英镑）。

背景知识

Uber：优步，是美国硅谷的一家科技公司。优步由加利福尼亚大学洛杉矶分校辍学学生特拉维斯·卡兰尼克和好友加勒特·坎普于2009年联合创立，因旗下同名打车APP而名声大噪。优步目前已在全球范围内覆盖了70多个国家的400余座城市。

生词点睛

ride-hailing service 叫车服务	**subsidise** v. 补助；补贴
rival n. 敌手	**monopoly** n. 垄断

重点表达

- **squeeze out** 排挤；挤出

Latin and Greek will be **squeezed out** of school timetables. 拉丁语和希腊语将退出学校的课程表。

- **pay a heavy price** 付出沉重的代价

If the polarization between the rich and the poor continues, the country will **pay a heavy** social and political **price**. 如果贫富继续两极分化，这个国家将会付出惨重的社会和政治代价。

Para. 2 Across Britain, gig work—part of a casualised, precarious and on-call jobs market—is growing at a giddy rate. The sector has more than doubled in size since 2016 and now accounts for 4.7 million workers. In part this is due to new technology: people are using apps on their mobile phones to sell their labour. Uncertain work is becoming the norm, with the result that unemployment statistics look better than the way Britons feel.

译文 零工工作属于工作市场中临时、不稳定且需要随时待命的一类，英国各地的零工工作都在以令人眩目的速度增加着。零工工作者的规模自2016年以来已经翻了一倍，现已达到470万人。这一定程度上是由新科技的出现导致的：人们正在利用手机上的APP出卖自己的劳动力。从事多变的工作正成为常态，其结果是失业统计数据看上去比英国民众所感受到的要乐观。

生词点睛

gig work 零工	**precarious** adj. 不稳定的
on-call adj. 随叫随到的	**giddy** adj. 令人头晕目眩的
norm n. 常态；规范	

Para. 3 At present there are three categories of employment status in the UK: employee, worker and the self-employed. Only the first category is entitled to full employment rights, including redundancy payments, parental leave, and protection against unfair dismissal. The second category ought to have their minimum wage and trade union rights protected, as well as paid holiday entitlement. However, gig-economy firms assume their workers to be self-employed, and fight trade unions such as the Independent Workers' Union of Great Britain (IWGB) who claim otherwise. In almost every case workers in the gig economy have proved that they are in fact employees. It is absurd that judges must protect workers from forced self-employment.

译文 当前英国的就业状态细分为三种：雇员、工人、个体经营者。只有雇员享有完整的就业权，其中包括遣散补偿金、亲子假期以及不公平解雇保护等权益。工人的最低工资、工会权以及带薪假期理应得到保障。然而，依赖零工经济的企业认为其员工是个体经营者，并与在这一问题上持有不同意见的工会（如英国独立工人联盟）做斗争。几乎在所有情况下，零工工作者都证明自己实际上是属雇员一类。法官们必须保护员工不被强行算作个体经营者，这实属荒诞。

生词点睛

self-employed *adj.* 个体经营的	**redundancy** *n.* 多余；裁员
parental leave 亲子假	**dismissal** *n.* 解雇；开除；驳回
entitlement *n.* 权利，资格	**absurd** *adj.* 荒谬的

重点表达

❖ be entitled to sth. 具有某种权利

Women workers **are entitled to** maternity leave with full pay. 女工产假期间工资照发。

Para. 4 It ought to be possible for workers to have flexible work without denying them basic rights. Businesses can only compete fairly if employment rules are equally applied and consistently enforced. On a deeper level, the gig economy is erasing what was for many the traditional

译文 工作者们理应能在弹性工作的同时保有基本的权利。只有将各种雇佣规定平等且始终如一地落实，企业才能公平竞争。从更深的层面而言，零工经济正在抹除人们通过工作想要实现的传统目标：换取自由支配

goal of working: to buy free time. Instead we are being seduced and coerced into thinking that it is good to commercialise our leisure time and possessions. Unless we can turn away from such thinking, we shall see ourselves acting less like humans and more like companies.

的时间。相反，它正通过威逼利诱让我们认为，把自己的闲暇时间和财产商品化是件好事。我们必须摒弃这种思想，否则我们将会发现自己的行为越来越不像人类而更像企业。

生词点睛

consistently adv. 持续地	**seduce** v. 诱惑
coerce v. 强迫；迫使	**commercialise** v. 使商品化
possession n. 财产；财富	

重点表达

❖ deny sb. sth. 拒绝给予某人某事物

His ex-wife **denies him access** to their children. 前妻拒绝让他接近他们的孩子。

❖ turn away from 远离；背离

Don't **turn away from** your conscience. 不要违背自己的良心。

• 词意选选看 •

1. subsidise ____   a. 权利
2. rival ____   b. 诱惑
3. monopoly ____   c. 补贴
4. norm ____   d. 对手
5. entitlement ____   e. 垄断
6. absurd ____   f. 强迫
7. consistently ____   g. 荒谬的
8. seduce ____   h. 常态
9. coerce ____   i. 财产
10. possession ____   j. 持续地

> ·拓展阅读·

零工经济

In a gig economy, businesses save resources in terms of benefits, office space and training. They also have the ability to contract with experts for specific projects who might be too high-priced to maintain on staff. From the perspective of the freelancer, a gig economy can improve work-life balance over what is possible in most jobs. Ideally, the model is powered by independent workers selecting jobs that they're interested in, rather than one in which people are forced into a position where, unable to attain employment, they pick up whatever temporary gigs they can land.

延伸思考：零工经济的盛行与共享经济有何关联？

第 2 天

Some fascinating Google Docs have been making the rounds lately—spreadsheets where people in various industries share how much they're being paid. "Talking about how much or how little money you make feels taboo, and it shouldn't," begins one document.

This is not just a matter of curiosity: Having greater access to salary information is helping speed things up. A new research report by the American Association of University Women shows that the wage gap tends to be smaller in job sectors where pay transparency is mandatory: For example, among federal government workers, there's just 13 percent pay disparity between men and women, and in state government, it's about 17 percent. In private, for-profit companies, where salaries are generally kept under wraps, that number jumps to 29 percent.

For far too long, sharing how much you're paid has been off-limits, kind of like talking about what you weigh. But that culture of secrecy makes pay discrepancies difficult to detect. If employees aren't aware of who's earning what, it's hard to know when someone—a woman, for instance, or a person of color—is being shortchanged.

For a generation accustomed to sharing their lives on social media, though, the idea of talking about salaries isn't much of a stretch. What's more, salary information is increasingly available on websites like Salary.com and Glassdoor. Other employers share salary bands, so their workers can know the compensation range for a particular position. And many human resources departments are providing that information for anyone who asks.

Laws are changing, too. Around the country, states have been passing equal pay provisions that prevent employers from forbidding or punishing workers for sharing salary information with their colleagues—a practice that until recently was far too common. Currently, 20 states have laws that ban retaliation for disclosing salaries. And the federal Paycheck Fairness Act, a pay equity bill that was recently passed by the House of Representatives and is awaiting action in the Senate, would also protect employees who want to share information about their earnings.

Of course, it's going to take more than salary transparency to equalize earnings between women and men. Women's work has long been undervalued, and they continue to face barriers and biases that hinder their earning power. But sharing salaries can be part of the solution: The more information women have about how jobs are valued—and what different people earn—the better they will understand their value in the labor market and push for the pay they deserve.

专题四 政策与民生

·文章大意·

第一段：分享薪资信息的文档正在网上流传。

第二、三段：分享薪资有利于减小两性收入差距；而薪资保密则让员工难以发现收入差异的存在。

第四段：部分雇员、第三方网站以及雇主已采取不同方式来促进薪资信息的透明化。

第五段：各地政府也在出台相关法规以保障员工讨论和分享薪资信息的权利。

第六段：薪资透明化能在一定程度上帮助解决两性收入不平等的问题。

·逐段精讲·

Para. 1 Some fascinating Google Docs have been making the rounds lately—spreadsheets where people in various industries share how much they're being paid. "Talking about how much or how little money you make feels taboo, and it shouldn't," begins one document.

译文 一些有趣的谷歌文档最近正在网上广为流传——各行各业的人们都在这些电子表格中分享自己的收入情况。其中一份文档的开头写道："谈论自己的收入高低被人们视为禁忌，但情况本不该如此。"

生词点睛

| **spreadsheet** n. 电子表格 | **taboo** n. 禁忌 |

重点表达

❖ make the rounds 巡逻；巡回

Whenever we go back to the place where my wife was born, we always have to **make the rounds** of her relatives. 每次去我妻子的老家，我们都得一家一家地走亲戚。

Para. 2 This is not just a matter of curiosity: Having greater access to salary information is helping speed things up. A new research report by the American Association of University Women shows that the wage gap tends to be smaller in job sectors where pay transparency is mandatory: For example, among federal government workers, there's just 13 percent pay disparity between men and women, and in state government, it's about 17 percent. In private, for-profit companies, where salaries are generally kept under wraps, that number jumps to 29 percent.

译文 谈论薪资不仅仅是为了满足好奇心：接触更多的薪资信息可以促进一些事情的发展。美国大学女性协会发布的一份报告表明，在收入必须透明化的行业里，工资差距往往更小：例如，就联邦政府的员工而言，男女薪资差距仅为13%，在州政府中大约为17%。而在薪酬情况通常保密的营利性私企中，这一数字则高达29%。

生词点睛

transparency *n.* 透明度	**mandatory** *adj.* 强制的
federal *adj.* 联邦的	**disparity** *n.* 差异；不同

重点表达

❖ speed up sth. 使加速
The new system should **speed up** the traffic flow. 新系统应该可以加快交通流速。

❖ under wraps 处于保密状态
You can never keep an event as big as ours completely **under wraps**. 像我们这么大规模的活动，要绝对保密是不可能的。

Para. 3 For far too long, sharing how much you're paid has been off-limits, kind of like talking about what you weigh. But that culture of secrecy makes pay discrepancies difficult to detect. If employees aren't aware of who's earning what, it's hard to know when someone—a woman, for instance, or **a person of color**—is being shortchanged.

译文 长期以来，分享自己的收入情况一直是种忌讳，这有点类似于谈论自己的体重。但这种保密文化使得人们难以察觉收入差异。如果员工们不了解各自到底赚了多少钱，也就很难知道某个人——比如女性或有色人种——正在遭受亏待。

背景知识

a person of color: 有色人种,一般被欧美社会定义为除白人以外的所有人种,包括黑人、黄种人、拉丁人、印度人,还有白人与其他种族混血人。

生词点睛

off-limits *adj.* 禁止的	**secrecy** *n.* 保密
discrepancy *n.* 差异;不一致	**shortchange** *v.* 偷工减料;缺斤少两

重点表达

❖ be aware of 意识到

Be aware of the terrible strain it can bring about when you expect the best result. 在期盼自己能取得最好的结果时,要当心这种心态带来的巨大压力。

Para. 4 For a generation accustomed to sharing their lives on social media, though, the idea of talking about salaries isn't much of a stretch. What's more, salary information is increasingly available on websites like Salary.com and Glassdoor. Other employers share salary bands, so their workers can know the compensation range for a particular position. And many human resources departments are providing that information for anyone who asks.

译文 不过对于我们这一代习惯了在社交媒体上分享自己生活的人来说,谈论薪水其实并非难事。而且,通过Salary和Glassdoor这样的网站,薪资信息的获取也变得越发容易了。一些雇主会公开薪资等级,其员工可以通过这种方式了解特定职位的工资范围。还有很多公司的人力资源部门会为任何前来询问的员工提供相关薪资信息。

生词点睛

stretch *n.* 拉伸;困难的任务	**compensation** *n.* 报酬;补偿金

重点表达

❖ be accustomed to sth. 适应某事

They have to learn how to **be accustomed to** a new environment and how to get along with the teachers and classmates. 他们要学会如何适应新的环境以及如何与老师和同学相处。

Para. 5　Laws are changing, too. Around the country, states have been passing equal pay provisions that prevent employers from forbidding or punishing workers for sharing salary information with their colleagues—a practice that until recently was far too common. Currently, 20 states have laws that ban retaliation for disclosing salaries. And the federal Paycheck Fairness Act, a pay equity bill that was recently passed by **the House of Representatives** and is awaiting action in **the Senate**, would also protect employees who want to share information about their earnings.

译文　相关法律也在改变。全国各州已经通过了多种同工同酬的法规，以防雇主禁止员工与同事分享薪资信息或因此惩罚他们，这类做法此前极为常见。目前已有 20 个州立法禁止了针对薪资披露的报复行为。而最近刚刚在众议院通过，尚待参议院审议的《联邦工资公平法案》届时也将保护那些想要分享收入信息的员工。

背景知识

the House of Representatives（众议院）、the Senate（参议院）：两院制是一些西方国家设上院下院并立，分担议会职能的制度。两院制最初产生于 17 世纪的英国，后为其他国家所广泛采用。其名称各有不同，如英国叫上议院（贵族院）和下议院（平民院）；美国、日本叫参议院和众议院；法国叫参议院和国民议会等。

生词点睛

provision *n.* 规定	**practice** *n.* 做法
retaliation *n.* 报复	**disclose** *v.* 披露
act *n.* 法案	**equity** *v.* 公平；股东资产

Para. 6 Of course, it's going to take more than salary transparency to equalize earnings between women and men. Women's work has long been undervalued, and they continue to face barriers and biases that hinder their earning power. But sharing salaries can be part of the solution: The more information women have about how jobs are valued—and what different people earn—the better they will understand their value in the labor market and push for the pay they deserve.

译文 当然，要想使两性收入平等，光靠薪资透明是不够的。社会长期以来都低估了女性工作的价值，她们还要不断面对种种阻碍她们赚钱的障碍与歧视。但分享薪资信息至少能解决一部分问题：女性对各种工作以及各类人的收入信息掌握得越多，就越有利于她们理解自己在劳动力市场上的价值并去争取应得的薪水。

生词点睛

undervalue *v.* 低估	**barrier** *n.* 障碍
hinder *v.* 妨碍	**labor market** 劳动力市场

重点表达

❖ push for sth. 奋力争取

It is a time to strengthen oversight, improve governance and **push for** freer and more efficient markets. 现在正是加强监督、改善治理，以及努力营造更加自由、高效的市场的时候。

词意选选看

1. taboo ____   a. 差异
2. transparency ____   b. 规定
3. federal ____   c. 禁忌
4. discrepancy ____   d. 障碍
5. stretch ____   e. 做法
6. compensation ____   f. 联邦的
7. provision ____   g. 拉伸
8. practice ____   h. 透明度

9. barrier _____
10. hinder _____

i. 妨碍
j. 补偿金

·拓展阅读·

对"同工同酬"的批评

　　Some believe that government actions to correct gender pay disparity serve to interfere with the system of voluntary exchange. They argue the fundamental issue is that the employer is the owner of the job, not the government or the employee. The employer negotiates the job and pays according to performance, not according to job duties. The issue with that is men are perceived to be high performers based on the same skill that a woman would have been able to do.

延伸思考：是否应该推行"同工同酬"？

第3天

The Conservative Party manifesto promised that when the party was in power it would charge foreign buyers of homes in England an extra 3% on the purchase price in stamp duty. Such taxes have been used in Canada, Singapore and Australia to tackle housing crises. However, no mention was made of the charge in the Queen's speech. If it does not pop up in the budget the Conservatives would have missed a chance to show they understand how voters feel crowded out of the housing market while wealthy overseas buyers are crowded in.

Estate agents say the proportion of homes in England and Wales let by overseas-based landlords rose to 11% during the first 10 months of 2019, the first year-on-year increase since 2010. Nearly one in five of London's homes are rented out by people not based in the UK. The trend is not just visible in the capital. The east of England recorded the biggest jumps in the number of overseas landlords. People say they are being priced out of living in Manchester because of foreign cash.

It is wrong for property to be seen purely as a financial product yielding a return when voters cannot afford homes for themselves. There is a wider cultural unease that needs to be appreciated. The phenomenon that needs to be countered is that ordinary people are losing ground to a wealthy elite. Some rich people just buy property and then leave it empty. This is the absurdity of rows of "ghost houses" in London at a time when the living cannot afford to put a roof above their head in the capital.

In a globalised and hyper-commercialised world, some think it is fine that everything has its price. That logic leads one to say that if a foreign billionaire can pay more than a local can, he or she should be able to whatever the consequences. This is a poor view of the sort of society we should want.

What is a concern is that, in a packed list of housing announcements in December, ministers avoided any measures that would have had a real impact on the UK housing crisis. There were no house building targets. No mention of social housing. There needs to be less glorification of power and money and more thought given to the wellbeing and needs of citizens.

文章大意

第一段：保守党曾承诺掌权后会向海外房东征收印花税，但没有兑现承诺。

第二段：海外房东的比重在英国普遍呈上升趋势，对本地居民造成了负面影响。

第三段：海外富裕阶层买房空置，本地人却难觅栖身之所的情况必须改变。

第四段：不该单纯地将关乎民生的住房看作一种金融产品，任由金主购买而不加以限制。

第五段：面对当前的住房危机，英国政府仍未采取有效行动。政府应多为人民的福祉考虑。

逐段精讲

Para. 1 The Conservative Party manifesto promised that when the party was in power it would charge foreign buyers of homes in England an extra 3% on the purchase price in stamp duty. Such taxes have been used in Canada, Singapore and Australia to tackle housing crises. However, no mention was made of the charge in the Queen's speech. If it does not pop up in the budget the Conservatives would have missed a chance to show they understand how voters feel crowded out of the housing market while wealthy overseas buyers are crowded in.

译文 保守党在其政党宣言中承诺掌权后会向外国房产买家额外征收购买价3%的印花税。加拿大、新加坡和澳大利亚等国已通过征收此类税目来解决住房危机。然而，女王的演讲中并未提及征税问题。选民们正在被涌入的海外买家挤出房地产市场，如果这项税收没有出现在预算中的话，保守党就失去了一次对这些选民的遭遇表示感同身受的机会。

背景知识

the Conservative Party： 保守党，是英国议会第一大党，现任领袖为鲍里斯·约翰逊。保守党的支持者一般来自企业界和富裕阶层。保守党主张自由市场经济，严格控制货币供应量，减少公共开支，压低通货膨胀，限制工会权利，加强"法律"和"秩序"等。保守党还强调维护英国主权，反对"联邦欧洲"、欧盟制宪，不加入欧元区。

生词点睛

manifesto *n.* 宣言	**stamp duty** 印花税
pop up 突然出现	**voter** *n.* 选民

重点表达

❖ in power 掌权

They seem to make better proposals when they are out of office than when they are **in power**. 在野时他们似乎能比执政时提出更好的议案。

Para. 2 Estate agents say the proportion of homes in England and Wales let by overseas-based landlords rose to 11% during the first 10 months of 2019, the first year-on-year increase since 2010. Nearly one in five of London's homes are rented out by people not based in the UK. The trend is not just visible in the capital. The east of England recorded the biggest jumps in the number of overseas landlords. People say they are being priced out of living in Manchester because of foreign cash.

译文 房地产中介说，海外房东出租英格兰和威尔士房屋的比例在2019年的前十个月里增至11%，这是该数据自2010年以来首次出现同比增长。伦敦近五分之一的房子都被平时不住在英国的人出租了。这样的趋势不单单出现在首都。英格兰东部地区的海外房东数量出现了有史以来最大幅度的增加。人们表示，由于境外资本的影响，自己已经负担不起曼彻斯特的生活。

生词点睛

estate agent 房地产中介	**landlord** *n.* 房东
year-on-year increase 同比增长	**rent** *v.* 出租

重点表达

❖ be let by 被……出租

Many caravans **are let by** private individuals through ads in papers or shop windows. 许多旅行拖车由私人通过在报纸或商店橱窗上登广告出租。

❖ be priced out of sth. 负担不起……

We're reforming our system of higher education to give colleges more incentives to offer better value, so that no kid **is priced out of** a college education. 我们正在改革高等教育体系，以激励大学提供更有价值的教育，不会让任何一个孩子负担不起大学教育。

Para. 3 It is wrong for property to be seen purely as a financial product yielding a return when voters cannot afford homes for themselves. There is a wider cultural unease that needs to be appreciated. The phenomenon that needs to be countered is that ordinary people are losing ground to a wealthy elite. Some rich people just buy property and then leave it empty. This is the absurdity of rows of "ghost houses" in London at a time when the living cannot afford to put a roof above their head in the capital.

译文 当选民们仅靠自己已经买不起房的时候，我们不该把房产单纯地看作一种能产生经济回报的金融产品。有一种更广泛的文化上的不安需要获得理解。普通人"让位"于富裕精英阶层的现象需要得到遏止。一些富人买来房产后就放在那里空置。在本地居民没钱在首都栖身安家的当下，伦敦成排的"鬼屋"则显得非常荒诞。

生词点睛

property *n.* 财产	**purely** *adv.* 纯粹地
yield *v.* 产出	**unease** *n.* 不安
elite *n.* 精英	**row** *n.* 排；列

重点表达

❖ lose ground to sth. 让位于……；面对……节节败退

Foreign brands continue to **lose ground to** domestic brands and now account for only a little more than one-third of the market. 外国品牌在国产品牌面前节节败退，目前仅占中国市场略多于三分之一的市场份额。

Para. 4 In a globalised and hyper-commercialised world, some think it is fine that everything has its price. That logic leads one to say that if a foreign billionaire can pay more than a local can, he or she should be able to whatever the consequences. This is a poor view of the sort of society we should want.

译文 在这个全球化且高度商业化的世界里，有些人认为万物皆有定价是无可厚非的。按照这种逻辑，只要一个外国亿万富翁能比本地人出更多的钱买房，无论后果如何，他（她）就应该有这样做的权利。这可不是我们期待的理想社会景象。

生词点睛

hyper-commercialised *adj.* 高度商业化的	logic *n.* 逻辑

Para. 5 What is a concern is that, in a packed list of housing announcements in December, ministers avoided any measures that would have had a real impact on the UK housing crisis. There were no house building targets. No mention of social housing. There needs to be less glorification of power and money and more thought given to the wellbeing and needs of citizens.

译文 值得担心的是，面对十二月堆积如山的住房公告，大臣们仍然不愿意采取任何能有效应对住房危机的措施。政府没有房屋建设目标，也没提及保障性住房。政府应该对权力和金钱少些赞扬，对人民的幸福与需求多些考虑。

生词点睛

packed *adj.* 大量的；挤满的	announcement *n.* 公告
glorification *n.* 赞颂，赞扬	

重点表达

❖ make no mention of sth. 没有提及……

The statement **made no mention of** civilian casualties. 公告里没有提及平民伤亡情况。

• 词意选选看 •

1. manifesto _____
2. voter _____
3. estate agent _____
4. rent _____
5. property _____
6. purely _____
7. yield _____
8. elite _____
9. row _____
10. logic _____

a. 纯粹地
b. 房地产中介
c. 排
d. 产出
e. 宣言
f. 逻辑
g. 选民
h. 出租
i. 财产
j. 精英

• 拓展阅读 •

英国的租房情况

　　Nearly two out of five households rent their home. However, the supply of rental properties has been declining since 2016 when the taxation treatment of rental property turned against landlords. Those in the upper half of the income distribution would typically rent a home while saving for a deposit to get onto the property ladder. This is no longer possible; money which would have been used in saving for a deposit now goes on rent. The majority of new households formed in the UK can now expect to rent from a private landlord for life. This phenomenon has been called generation rent.

延伸思考：充足的房屋供给对租房群体有何影响？

第 4 天

The restoration of maintenance grants for student nurses, starting next September, is a welcome signal that the government is capable of facing up to past mistakes. The 323,000 registered nurses working in the NHS in England are the biggest staff group (there are 146,000 doctors). While staff shortages are an issue across the service—and increasingly understood not only as a national issue but as a global one—predictions that the current figure of 43,000 NHS nursing vacancies could rise to almost 70,000 by 2023-2024 have clearly focused minds.

Without qualified staff, hospitals and health trusts cannot function properly. But the new £5,000-a-year grant should be viewed as an important first step on a longer road to improving nursing, and not as a final destination. Retention of staff is just as important as recruitment, since there is not much point in training and hiring people if you cannot hold on to them. The national nursing staff turnover rate has fallen from 12.5% to 11.9% over the past two years, and a rise in the number of registered nurses and midwives also offers some grounds for hope. But there are worrying trends too, including an aging workforce, and the stream of departures of nurses from other parts of the EU.

The challenge to the health system overall from the combination of underfunding and an aging population with increasingly complex health needs, including a much higher incidence of chronic illness, is widely acknowledged. The 2012 Health and Social Care Act is widely seen to have made a difficult situation worse. But the impact of all this on nursing careers requires closer attention. Numbers are not the be-all and end-all, as health researchers such as Alison Leary have argued, and the approach to workforce planning taken by management accountants does not sit easily with the sheer human complexity of much healthcare work. While the number of "assistive" healthcare roles is rising, the extent to which senior nurses withdraw from frontline caregiving should be reviewed.

People are grateful when they are treated kindly. But we do patients, as well as staff, a disservice if we reduce nursing to handing out pills and holding hands. The return of grants for training should be viewed as more than a sticking plaster. Along with the restoration of budgets for later professional development, it should be viewed as a vital investment in a national human resource.

文章大意

第一段：英国实习护士的生活补助金即将恢复，这有助于缓解英国医护人员短缺的现状。

第二段：恢复实习护士的补助金只是解决医护问题的第一步，后续的人员留存问题也同样重要。

第三段：资金不足以及人口老龄化使医疗系统面临很大的压力，过去相关法案的制定没有充分考虑到医护工作的复杂性，所以使得这一问题雪上加霜。

第四段：医护人员数量的多少对患者来说意义重大，恢复补助金不仅是为了解医护人员短缺的燃眉之急，其更是一笔重要的人力资源投资。

逐段精讲

Para. 1 The restoration of maintenance grants for student nurses, starting next September, is a welcome signal that the government is capable of facing up to past mistakes. The 323,000 registered nurses working in the NHS in England are the biggest staff group (there are 146,000 doctors). While staff shortages are an issue across the service—and increasingly understood not only as a national issue but as a global one—predictions that the current figure of 43,000 NHS nursing vacancies could rise to almost 70,000 by 2023-2024 have clearly focused minds.

译文 九月起实习护士的生活补助金即将恢复，这是一个积极的信号，意味着政府能正视过去犯下的错误了。英国医疗服务体系内在编的 323 000 名护士是英国最大的员工群体（医生有 146 000 人）。医护人员短缺是医疗服务行业的一大问题，并且人们越发意识到这不仅是本国的问题，更是一个全球性的问题；预测英国医疗服务体系目前 43 000 名的医护缺口到 2023 年或 2024 年将达到近 70 000 人，这无疑引起了人们的关注。

生词点睛

restoration *n.* 恢复	**grant** *n.* 拨款
register *v.* 注册	**vacancy** *n.* 空缺

Para. 2 Without qualified staff, hospitals and health trusts cannot function properly. But the new £5,000-a-year grant should be viewed as an important first step on a longer road to improving nursing, and not as a final destination. Retention of staff is just as important as recruitment, since there is not much point in training and hiring people if you cannot hold on to them. The national nursing staff turnover rate has fallen from 12.5% to 11.9% over the past two years, and a rise in the number of registered nurses and midwives also offers some grounds for hope. But there are worrying trends too, including an aging workforce, and the stream of departures of nurses from other parts of the EU.

译文 没有具备资质的员工，医院和健康信托基金就无法正常运作。但我们应该把5 000英镑一年的新拨款视作改善医护情况的万里长征的第一步而非终点。员工的留存跟招聘同等重要，因为如果无法留住员工的话，培训和雇用他们就毫无意义了。过去的两年里，全国医护人员的流失率从12.5%下降到了11.9%，在编护士和助产护士人数的上升也给我们带来了些许希望。但也存在一些令人担心的趋势，包括劳动力的老龄化以及欧盟其他国家护士的离职潮。

生词点睛

trust *n.* 信托基金	**retention** *n.* 留存
turnover rate 流失率；周转率	**midwife** *n.* 助产士
stream *n.* （人）流	**departure** *n.* 离开

重点表达

❖ there is no point in sth. 某事毫无意义

There is no point in pushing them unless they are talented and they enjoy it. 除非他们很有才华而且自己喜欢，否则逼迫他们是没有意义的。

Para. 3 The challenge to the health system overall from the combination of underfunding and an aging population with increasingly complex health needs, including a much higher incidence of chronic illness, is widely acknowledged. The 2012 Health and Social Care

译文 人们普遍认为，资金不足和人口老龄化（老龄人口的医疗需求日益复杂，慢性病发病率很高），共同对医疗系统构成了挑战；《2012年健康与社

Act is widely seen to have made a difficult situation worse. But the impact of all this on nursing careers requires closer attention. Numbers are not the be-all and end-all, as health researchers such as Alison Leary have argued, and the approach to workforce planning taken by management accountants does not sit easily with the sheer human complexity of much healthcare work. While the number of "assistive" healthcare roles is rising, the extent to which senior nurses withdraw from frontline caregiving should be reviewed.

会保障法案》使得这一问题雪上加霜。但需要密切关注这一切对护士的职业生涯的影响。正如像艾丽森·利里等健康研究人员所说，数据并不是全部，管理会计师们制定劳动力计划时考虑不到大部分医护工作中人工的极端复杂性。虽然"助理"医护人员的数量正在增加，但资深护士从看护前线辞职的情况也应该得到检视。

生词点睛

underfunding *n.* 资金不足	**incidence** *n.* 概率
chronic *adj.* 慢性的	**accountant** *n.* 会计师
sheer *adj.* 纯粹的；十足的	**assistive** *adj.* 辅助性的

重点表达

❖ **the be-all and end-all** 全部；唯一重要的东西

Not everybody agreed that winning was **the be-all and end-all**. 并不是每个人都认为赢是最重要的。

❖ **withdraw from sth.** 从……退出、撤退

A back injury forced her to **withdraw from** Wimbledon. 背部受伤使她不得不退出温布尔登赛事。

Para. 4 People are grateful when they are treated kindly. But we do patients, as well as staff, a disservice if we reduce nursing to handing out pills and holding hands. The return of grants for training should be viewed as more than a sticking plaster.

译文 受到体贴的照顾时，人们便会感恩。但如果减少负责发放药品并给予患者精神支持的护士的数量，我们就是在伤害患者和护士。恢复实习护士的补助金起到的不仅是创可贴救

Along with the restoration of budgets for later professional development, it should be viewed as a vital investment in a national human resource.

急的作用。随着后续职业发展的预算资金的恢复，该补助金应该被视为国家人力资源领域的一笔关键投资。

生词点睛

grateful *adj.* 感激的	**patient** *n.* 患者
disservice *n.* 损害；伤害	**pill** *n.* 药丸
sticking plaster 创可贴	**vital** *adj.* 极为关键的

重点表达

❖ hand out sth. 分发；发放

Planning permission **is handed out** sparingly. 建筑许可证的发放是很谨慎的。

词意选选看

1. restoration ____
2. grant ____
3. register ____
4. trust ____
5. stream ____
6. departure ____
7. chronic ____
8. sheer ____
9. patient ____
10. vital ____

a. 信托资金
b. 恢复
c. 离开
d. 拨款
e. 极为关键的
f. 注册
g. 患者
h. 慢性的
i. （人）流
j. 纯粹的

拓展阅读

医护人员的职业压力

The fast-paced and unpredictable nature of health care places nurses at risk for injuries and illnesses, including high occupational stress. Nursing is a particularly stressful profession, and nurses consistently identify stress as a major work-related concern and have among the highest levels of occupational stress when compared to other professions. This stress is caused by the environment, psychosocial stressors, and the demands of nursing, including new technology that must be mastered, the emotional labor involved in nursing, physical labor, shift work, and high workload. This stress puts nurses at risk of developing compassion fatigue and moral distress, which can worsen mental health.

延伸思考：如何有效缓解医护人员的压力？

第 5 天

International Women's Day, on 8 March, is like an annual progress report on women's rights, asking how far we have come. The findings of the UN Development Forum gender index, published on Thursday, provide a bleak answer: 90% of the population in 75 countries is biased against women. Meanwhile men's rights activists, living in a parallel universe they deem "gynocentric", believe "the efforts to enhance the rights of women have become toxic efforts to undermine the rights of men".

This kind of narrative has been around for more than 30 years. Starting with fathers angry about custody rights, it mutated into an extreme men's rights movement with distinctive male supremacist characteristics. More recently it entered the mainstream, overlapping with white supremacists.

They see rights as a zero-sum game, as if there existed only a limited pool of them, and if women gain more then men must inevitably have fewer. If women are now entering higher education in greater numbers than men, it must be because they've elbowed out the men. The shift from manufacturing to service isn't a macroeconomic and transnational trend but a plot by women—a "war on masculinity". There's even an International Men's Day.

The idea that women's rights are gained at the expense of men's is actually the opposite of the truth: there's now a stack of evidence that men benefit from living in more gender-equal societies and that policies promoting gender equality improve the quality of life of everyone, not just for women. A recent WHO report comparing 41 European countries found that men's health was poorer in more gender-unequal societies—the sexual division of labour harms men as well as women. When the sexes are more equal, men say they're more satisfied with life. In more gender-equal societies such as the Nordic countries, apparently both men and women sleep better. The latter, a finding from a recent European study, suggests that this isn't just because stresses affect our sleep but also because men in more equal societies take better care of themselves.

Before we rush into a gender-equal sexual nirvana, though, we need to factor in some other truths. Like the fact that most men benefit from male privilege and are unlikely to relinquish it voluntarily for some promised future gain. What's more, just as women don't form a single homogeneous group, neither do men: it's hard to see what privileges an unemployed man with a disability could trade in for a good night's sleep.

文章大意

第一、二段：当前世界上的性别不平等以及性别歧视问题较为严重。有人认为女权是以削弱男权为代价的，这种想法已成为社会主流。

第三段：持这种想法的人将权利视作一种零和博弈，认为任何不利于男性的事都是女性的阴谋。

第四段：然而大量研究表明，生活在性别更加平等的社会中对男性也是有益的。

第五段：社会需要认真思考如何让男性自愿放弃既得特权的问题。

逐段精讲

Para. 1 International Women's Day, on 8 March, is like an annual progress report on women's rights, asking how far we have come. The findings of the UN Development Forum gender index, published on Thursday, provide a bleak answer: 90% of the population in 75 countries is biased against women. Meanwhile men's rights activists, living in a parallel universe they deem "gynocentric", believe "the efforts to enhance the rights of women have become toxic efforts to undermine the rights of men".

译文 每年3月8号的国际妇女节就好像是一份女性权利的年度进展报告，询问我们究竟取得了多少进展。周四在联合国发展论坛上公布的性别指数给出的答案很不乐观：75个国家中90%的人口对女性抱有偏见。与此同时，激进的男权运动者还活在另一个平行宇宙里，在他们的"大女子主义"的世界中，增进女权的努力是削弱男权的毒瘤。

生词点睛

annual *adj.* 年度的	**forum** *n.* 论坛
bleak *adj.* 黯淡的	**parallel** *adj.* 平行的
deem *v.* 视为；认为	**undermine** *v.* 削弱

Para. 2 This kind of narrative has been around for more than 30 years. Starting with fathers angry about custody rights, it mutated into an extreme men's rights movement with distinctive male supremacist characteristics. More recently it entered the mainstream, overlapping with white supremacists.

译文 这种论调30年多年来一直存在。其发源于父亲们对监护权的愤怒，现在已经变异成一种具有明显的男性至上主义特质的极端男权运动。最近这种论调更是与白人至上主义混杂在一起，成了主流观点。

生词点睛

narrative *n.* 叙事	**custody** *n.* 监护；拘押
mutate *v.* 变异；转变	**supremacist** *n.* 至上主义者
mainstream *n.* 主流	**overlap** *v.* 重叠

重点表达

❖ be around 在附近

They can always **be around** whenever you need them. 你需要他们的时候，他们总能陪在你身边。

Para. 3 They see rights as a zero-sum game, as if there existed only a limited pool of them, and if women gain more then men must inevitably have fewer. If women are now entering higher education in greater numbers than men, it must be because they've elbowed out the men. The shift from manufacturing to service isn't a macroeconomic and transnational trend but a plot by women—a "war on masculinity". There's even an International Men's Day.

译文 他们将权利的争取视作一种零和博弈，好像权利的总量有限，一旦女性得到的权利变多了，那男性的权利就势必变少。如果当前接受高等教育的女性数量比男性多的话，那一定是因为她们挤占了男性的名额。从制造业到服务业的转型并不是宏观经济以及国际层面的趋势，而是女性的阴谋——是一场"针对男子气概的战争"。甚至还有一个国际男子节。

生词点睛

zero-sum game 零和博弈	**inevitably** *adv.* 不可避免地
elbow out 排挤；挤开	**transnational** *adj.* 跨国的
plot *n.* 阴谋；密谋	**masculinity** *n.* 男性；男子气概

重点表达

❖ a limited pool of sth. 很有限的……

There is **a limited pool of** people with the skills and qualifications to manage such a fund-raising. 缺少有能力和有资格的人来管理这场融资。

Para. 4 The idea that women's rights are gained at the expense of men's is actually the opposite of the truth: there's now a stack of evidence that men benefit from living in more gender-equal societies and that policies promoting gender equality improve the quality of life of everyone, not just for women. A recent **WHO** report comparing 41 European countries found that men's health was poorer in more gender-unequal societies—the sexual division of labour harms men as well as women. When the sexes are more equal, men say they're more satisfied with life. In more gender-equal societies such as the Nordic countries, apparently both men and women sleep better. The latter, a finding from a recent European study, suggests that this isn't just because stresses affect our sleep but also because men in more equal societies take better care of themselves.

译文 这种认为加强女权总是以牺牲男权为代价的想法实际上与事实相反：如今大量证据表明，生活在性别更加平等的社会中对男性是有益的，促进性别平等的政策能够提高所有人的生活质量，而不仅限于女性。世界卫生组织最近的一项报告比较了41个欧洲国家的情况，该报告发现在性别更加不平等的社会中，男性的健康情况也更差——劳动力的性别分化对男性和女性都会造成伤害。在性别更加平等的情况下，男人表示他们对生活更满意。在像北欧国家这样性别平等度更高的社会中，男性和女性的睡眠质量都明显更高。这份来自欧洲的最新研究表明，这不仅是因为压力影响睡眠，还因为在性别更加平等的社会中男性能更好地照顾自己。

专题四　政策与民生

背景知识

WHO：世界卫生组织（World Health Organization），是联合国下属的一个专门机构，总部设在瑞士日内瓦，是国际上最大的政府间卫生组织。其主要职能包括：促进流行病和地方病的防治；提供和改进公共卫生、疾病医疗和有关事项的教学与训练；推动确定生物制品的国际标准。

生词点睛

stack *n.* 一摞；许多	Nordic *adj.* 北欧的
apparently *adv.* 显然	

重点表达

❖ at the expense of sth. 以……为代价

You shouldn't be generous **at the expense of** others. 你不能慷他人之慨。

Para. 5 Before we rush into a gender-equal sexual nirvana, though, we need to factor in some other truths. Like the fact that most men benefit from male privilege and are unlikely to relinquish it voluntarily for some promised future gain. What's more, just as women don't form a single homogeneous group, neither do men: it's hard to see what privileges an unemployed man with a disability could trade in for a good night's sleep.

译文　不过在我们匆忙进入性别平等的极乐世界之前，我们还需要考虑其他一些事实。比如说大部分男性都得益于男性特权，且不会为了未来的某些收益而自愿放弃这种特权。此外，正如女性无法形成统一战线一样，男性也同样做不到：很难想象一个失业的残疾男性可以拿什么样的特权去换一晚的安眠。

生词点睛

rush *v.* 匆忙行事；快速移动	nirvana *n.* 涅槃；极乐世界
relinquish *v.*（不情愿地）放弃	homogeneous *adj.* 同种类的

重点表达

❖ trade in A for B 用 A 换取 B

I **trade in** my car **for** a new model. 我把自己的旧汽车卖了，换了一辆新车。

词意选选看

1. annual _____
2. bleak _____
3. deem _____
4. custody _____
5. mutate _____
6. mainstream _____
7. plot _____
8. masculinity _____
9. forum _____
10. homogeneous _____

a. 变异
b. 论坛
c. 男子气概
d. 年度的
e. 密谋
f. 视作
g. 同类的
h. 拘押
i. 主流
j. 黯淡的

拓展阅读

女权主义运动

Feminist movements have campaigned and continue to campaign for women's rights, including the right to vote, to hold public office, to work, to earn fair wages, equal pay and eliminate the gender pay gap, to own property, to receive education, to enter contracts, to have equal rights within marriage, and to have maternity leave. Feminists have also worked to ensure access to legal abortions and social integration and to protect women and girls from rape, sexual harassment, and domestic violence. Changes in dress and acceptable physical activity have often been part of feminist movements.

延伸思考：女权主义运动争取的权益有何内在共同点？

第 6 天

As the costs of college have climbed, some students have gone hungry. When they've voiced frustration, they've often been ridiculed: "Ramen is cheap," or "Just eat cereal."

But the blight of food insecurity among college students is real, and a new report from the Government Accountability Office (GAO), a nonpartisan congressional watchdog, highlights the breadth of those affected. There are potentially millions of students at risk of being food insecure, which means they do not have access to nutritious, affordable food, the report says. It is the first time the federal government has acknowledged food insecurity on campus in a significant way. The federal government spends billions of dollars on higher education each year, and this report finds that some students are at risk of dropping out because they cannot eat, although there aren't good data on just how many.

One chief way that campuses have been addressing hunger is by building food pantries on campus, but Sara Goldrick-Rab, a higher-education professor at Temple University and a leading scholar on campus hunger, told me that those only scratch the surface of the issue.

The government can address this issue systemically through the Supplemental Nutrition Assistance Program (snap, commonly known as food stamps), the report says, but it adds that "almost 2 million at-risk students"—defined as students who are low income or first generation, are raising children, or have another, similar risk factor—didn't receive snap benefits in 2016, even though they potentially could have.

That could be because those students didn't know they were eligible: The government restricts students who attend college at least half-time from receiving the benefits, but certain students are exempt from that restriction. The information that most schools and snap offices provide students about the program is shoddy, says Samuel Chu, a national organizer for Mazon, an advocacy organization focused on eradicating hunger. "There are very specific ways and accessible ways that students can access snap," he says, but even local snap offices are often unaware. For example, students who meet the basic criteria for snap eligibility and are younger than 18 or older than 50, or who have children, or who work a minimum of 20 hours a week are also eligible to receive the benefit. The GAO begged the Food and Nutrition Service, which administers snap, to improve information about student eligibility and share that information with its local offices.

Naturally, the report focuses heavily on low-income students, as they are perhaps those most likely to experience food insecurity. But Goldrick-Rab notes that they aren't the only students who are going hungry. Middle-class students, those who are "too rich for Pell and too poor to afford college," struggle as well. And they may not be as likely to use things such as the food pantry.

文章大意

第一段：指出一些大学生正在挨饿。
第二段：指出该问题的真实性及严重性。
第三段：指出校园采取的方法不够深入。
第四段：指出政府的补充营养援助项目及其实施状况。
第五段：指出补充营养援助项目的弊端及改进方法。
第六段：再次强调大学生食物无保障问题的严重性（广泛性）。

逐段精讲

Para. 1 As the costs of college have climbed, some students have gone hungry. When they've voiced frustration, they've often been ridiculed: "Ramen is cheap," or "Just eat cereal."

译文 随着大学费用的攀升，一些学生开始挨饿。当他们表示失望时，他们经常会被嘲笑"拉面很便宜"或者"就吃麦片吧"。

生词点睛

climb v. 攀登；上升	voice v. 表示，表达，吐露（感情或意见）
frustration n. 挫败；阻挠	ridicule v. 嘲笑，奚落；讥笑
ramen n. 拉面	

Para. 2 But the blight of food insecurity among college students is real, and a new report from the **Government Accountability Office (GAO)**, a nonpartisan congressional watchdog, highlights the breadth of those affected. There are potentially millions of students at risk of being food insecure, which means they do not have access to nutritious, affordable food, the report says. It is the first time the federal government has acknowledged food insecurity on campus in a significant way. The federal government spends billions of dollars on higher education each year, and this report finds that some students are at risk of dropping out because they cannot eat, although there aren't good data on just how many.

译文 但是大学生食物无保障问题是真实存在的，一个无党派的国会监督机构——美国政府问责局的一项最新报告强调了受影响人群的广泛程度。该报告表示，可能有数百万的学生面临食物无保障的危机，这意味着他们不能食用营养丰富、价格合理的食物。这是联邦政府首次以非常重视的态度承认校园食物无保障问题。联邦政府每年在高等教育上投入数十亿美元，该报告发现，由于饥饿，一些学生正面临着辍学的风险，虽然还没有关于辍学人数的准确数据。

背景知识

Government Accountability Office (GAO)：美国政府问责局，美国国会的下属机构，负责调查、监督联邦政府的规划和支出，其前身是美国总审计局。该机构是一个独立机构，只对国会负责，以中立精神开展工作，主要职责是调查联邦政府如何花纳税人的钱。

生词点睛

blight *n.* （对局势、生活或环境）有害的事物，不利因素	**insecurity** *n.* 不安全；不牢靠
nonpartisan *adj.* 无党派的	**watchdog** *n.* 监察委员会
highlight *v.* 强调；突出	**nutritious** *adj.* 有营养的，滋养的
acknowledge *v.* 承认（属实）	**good** *adj.* 准确的

重点表达

❖ at risk of + doing / *n.* 有……风险

Now, hundreds of kinds of animals are **at risk of** dying out. 如今，数百种动物面临灭绝的危险。
The United Nations warns up to 13 million civilians are **at risk of** starvation. 联合国警示，超过 1 300 万民众在饱受饥饿的威胁。

❖ have access to sth. 有……的机会/权利

Yes, in our hotel all rooms **have access to** the Internet. 是的，我们每间房都能连接到因特网。

❖ It is the first time (that) + 现在完成时 这是首次……

It's the first time (that) the boy has spoken to a foreigner. 这是这个男孩第一次跟外国人说话。

Para. 3 One chief way that campuses have been addressing hunger is by building food pantries on campus, but Sara Goldrick-Rab, a higher-education professor at **Temple University** and a leading scholar on campus hunger, told me that those only scratch the surface of the issue.

译文 校园解决饥饿问题的一个主要方式是在校园里建立食品储藏室，但天普大学的高等教育教授、校园饥饿问题的知名学者萨拉·戈德里克·拉布告诉我，这些食品储藏室只触及了问题的表面。

背景知识

Temple University：天普大学（又名"坦普尔大学"），至今已有超过百年的历史，被列入"费城三大名校"（另外两所是宾夕法尼亚大学和德雷塞尔大学），也是宾夕法尼亚州"三大公立大学"之一。

生词点睛

| pantry n. 食品储藏室 | leading adj. 最重要的；一流的 |

重点表达

❖ scratch the surface 只触及问题的表面，蜻蜓点水

Oh, you're only **scratching the surface**. 你这还只是看到皮毛而已。
The man never **scratched the surface** of life. 他根本从未真正地活过。

Para. 4 The government can address this issue systemically through the **Supplemental Nutrition Assistance Program** (snap, commonly known as food stamps), the report says, but it adds that "almost 2 million at-risk students"—defined as students who are low income or first generation, are raising children, or have another, similar risk factor—didn't receive snap benefits in 2016, even though they potentially could have.

译文 报告指出，政府可以通过"补充营养援助项目"（snap，通常被称为粮食券）系统地解决这一问题，但同时又补充道，"将近二百万有风险的学生"——正在抚养孩子的低收入学生或作为家里的第一代学生，或有其他类似的风险因素的学生——在 2016 年没有享受到该项目带来的福利，即使他们本应该得到该福利。

背景知识

Supplemental Nutrition Assistance Program：补充营养援助项目，之前称为"粮食券计划"，在 1939 年就已建立，是联邦政府最主要的反饥饿项目，旨在为穷人家庭提供食品经济补贴，以保证每个穷人都不会饿肚子。进入 21 世纪，美国农业部将食品券体系纳入食品保障体系，不光让穷人吃饱，还保证让他们吃得安全、营养、健康。

生词点睛

supplemental *adj*. 补充的，增补的	**potentially** *adv*. 可能地，潜在地

重点表达

❖ even if 即使

We shouldn't slight anybody **even if** he's a nobody. 我们不应该轻视任何人，即使他是一个小人物。

Para. 5 That could be because those students didn't know they were eligible: The government restricts students who attend college at least half-time from receiving the benefits, but certain students are exempt from that restriction. The information

译文 可能是因为那些学生不知道他们符合该福利的条件：政府限制上大学半工半读的学生享受福利，但某些学生不受这种限制。一个致力于消除饥饿的倡导组织——Mazon 的组织

that most schools and snap offices provide students about the program is shoddy, says Samuel Chu, a national organizer for **Mazon**, an advocacy organization focused on eradicating hunger. "There are very specific ways and accessible ways that students can access snap," he says, but even local snap offices are often unaware. For example, students who meet the basic criteria for snap eligibility and are younger than 18 or older than 50, or who have children, or who work a minimum of 20 hours a week are also eligible to receive the benefit. The GAO begged the Food and Nutrition Service, which administers snap, to improve information about student eligibility and share that information with its local offices.

者塞缪尔·楚说，大多数学校和补充营养援助项目办公室提供给学生的关于该项目的信息是不可靠的。"学生们可以通过一些非常具体和方便的方式来参与该项目。"塞缪尔说。但即便是当地的补充营养援助项目办公室也常常不知情。例如，符合补充营养援助项目资格基本标准，且年龄在18岁以下或50岁以上，有孩子或每周工作至少20小时的学生也有资格获得该福利。美国政府问责局恳请管理补充营养援助项目的美国食品和营养服务局改善有关学生享受该福利的资格的信息，并将这些信息与当地的办公室共享。

背景知识

Mazon：“犹太人对饥饿的回应”，是美国的一个非营利组织，致力于消除美国和以色列各种信仰和背景的人的饥饿。在希伯来语中，"Mazon"的意思是"食物"或"生计"。

生词点睛

eligible *adj.* 合适的；符合条件的	**shoddy** *adj.* 假冒的；劣质的
advocacy *n.* 主张；拥护；辩护	**eradicate** *v.* 根除；消灭

重点表达

❖ restrict sb. from doing sth. 限制某人做某事

No organization or individual shall obstruct or **restrict** them **from joining** unions. 任何组织和个人不得阻挠或限制他们参加工会。

❖ be exempted from 被免除；得到豁免

Justifiable defense is the act **being exempted from** crimes. 正当防卫不属于犯罪行为。

❖ meet the criteria 符合条件

If you **meet the criteria**, then in theory there should be no problem. 如果你达到标准，理论上应该没有问题。

Para. 6 Naturally, the report focuses heavily on low-income students, as they are perhaps those most likely to experience food insecurity. But Goldrick-Rab notes that they aren't the only students who are going hungry. Middle-class students, those who are "too rich for Pell and too poor to afford college," struggle as well. And they may not be as likely to use things such as the food pantry.

译文 自然，这份报告的重点是低收入家庭的学生，因为他们最有可能遭遇食物无保障问题。但戈德里克·拉布指出，他们并不是唯一正在挨饿的学生。中产阶级的学生，即那些"在佩尔看来很有钱却负担不起大学学费的"学生，同样也在苦苦挣扎。他们可能连诸如食品储藏室这样的东西都无法使用。

生词点睛

| **experience** v. 遭受；经历 | **struggle** v. 挣扎；奋斗，努力 |

重点表达

❖ be likely to do sth. 可能做某事；很可能

The train **is likely to** be late. 这趟火车很可能晚点。

·词意选选看·

1. watchdog ____   a. 表达，吐露（感情或意见）
2. ridicule ____   b. 食品储藏室
3. voice ____   c. 承认（属实）
4. good ____   d. 根除；消灭
5. acknowledge ____   e. 嘲笑，奚落；讥笑
6. eligible ____   f. 合适的；符合条件的
7. pantry ____   g. 假冒的；劣质的

8. eradicate ____   h. 准确的
9. ramen ____   i. 拉面
10. shoddy ____   j. 监察委员会

> 拓展阅读

大学生食物无保障问题

Food insecurity is defined as limited or uncertain availability of nutritionally adequate and safe foods, and the ability to acquire such food in acceptable ways. It has been associated with depression, stress, trouble learning in the classroom, and poor health. Food insecurity among college students is an important public health concern that might have implications for academic performance, retention, and graduation rates. Universities that measure food insecurity among their students will be better positioned to advocate for policy changes at state and federal levels regarding college affordability and student financial assistance.

延伸思考：如何有效解决大学生食物无保障问题？

第 7 天

The introduction of compulsory health and relationships education in English primary schools should be applauded. Children are entitled to be informed about themselves, and the world, as part of their schooling. As well as the facts about bodies, minds, human differences and similarities, they should be taught to think about their feelings for other people. Parents, carers and wider networks of friends and relatives have a crucial role in socialising the next generation. But input from teachers and classmates is also essential. Schools are, in almost all cases, the place where young people start to make their way in the world as individuals, learn to manage themselves in a peer group, and separate from their families.

In many classrooms across the country, these kinds of lessons already happen, in both primary and secondary schools, under the PSHE (personal, social, health, and economic education) heading. It would have been preferable for the government to build on existing good practice by taking the simple step of making PSHE compulsory. But the new guidance from the Department for Education, which covers sex education in secondary schools as well as setting out what should be taught to primary-age children, is still a big step.

Since official guidance on sex education was last updated in 2000 there is, as the education secretary, Damian Hinds, has acknowledged, much catching up to do. In particular, the role of technology requires urgent attention. Schools already make efforts to promote online safety, by alerting parents to the risks posed by unsuitable content, and encouraging them to reflect on how much time children spend using screens. It makes sense to instruct children in such issues directly, and supply them with the tools to think about their behaviour.

The crisis in young people's mental health is well documented. It would be glib to suggest that revisions to the curriculum offer any kind of solution to a problem that has been out of control, and been greatly exacerbated by cuts to both national and local mental health services. But that is not to say that schools are helpless. It is a good idea to teach young people how to talk about their emotions, how to recognise symptoms of anxiety or depression, and how to access professional help.

As with the sensible package announced by Mr. Hinds last month to address teacher shortages, the devil of these proposals is in the details of their funding. None of what has been promised will be delivered to the required standard unless the government increases its paltry offer of £6m. Beyond the nuts and bolts of the facts of life, these are issues that require well-informed and sensitive handling: sexual orientation, gender identity, self-harm and abuse are deeply personal and difficult subjects to tackle in a classroom.

文章大意

第一段：开展健康与异性关系义务教育应该受到称赞。
第二段：PSHE 未成为义务课程。
第三段：教授孩子们这些问题是有意义的。
第四段：学校的教育起到了一定的作用。
第五段：资金问题阻碍了学校展开教育。

逐段精讲

Para. 1 The introduction of compulsory health and relationships education in English primary schools should be applauded. Children are entitled to be informed about themselves, and the world, as part of their schooling. As well as the facts about bodies, minds, human differences and similarities, they should be taught to think about their feelings for other people. Parents, carers and wider networks of friends and relatives have a crucial role in socialising the next generation. But input from teachers and classmates is also essential. Schools are, in almost all cases, the place where young people start to make their way in the world as individuals, learn to manage themselves in a peer group, and separate from their families.

译文 在英国小学开展健康与异性关系义务教育应该受到称赞。作为学校教育的一部分，儿童有权了解自己和整个世界。除了身体、思想、人类的异同等事实以外，他们还应该学会思考自己对他人的感受。父母、看护者和更广泛的亲友关系网在下一代的社交生活中扮演着关键角色。但从老师和同学那里学到的东西也很重要。在绝大部分情况下，学校是年轻人作为独立的个体开始探索世界的地方，是开始学习在同龄群体中管理自己、学习离开家庭独自生活的地方。

生词点睛

compulsory *adj.* 义务的；必修的	**applaud** *v.* 赞同；称赞
schooling *n.* 学校教育	**essential** *adj.* 必不可少的，绝对必要的；非常重要的
peer *n.* 同龄人；社会地位相同的人	

重点表达

❖ have (play) a crucial role in 在……中起关键作用

Parents **have a crucial role in** how their children develop as human beings. 家长在孩子的人格发展方面起着至关重要的作用。

Para. 2　In many classrooms across the country, these kinds of lessons already happen, in both primary and secondary schools, under the **PSHE** (personal, social, health, and economic education) heading. It would have been preferable for the government to build on existing good practice by taking the simple step of making PSHE compulsory. But the new guidance from the Department for Education, which covers sex education in secondary schools as well as setting out what should be taught to primary-age children, is still a big step.

译文　这类课程已出现在全国许多中小学的课堂上，属于个人、社会、健康和经济教育（简称 PSHE）范畴。政府在现有良好实践的基础上，采取简单步骤使 PSHE 成为义务课程本来会更好，但教育部的新指南仍然是一个很大的进步，新指南包括中学的性教育，并陈述了应该向小学生讲授的内容。

背景知识

PSHE："个人、社会、健康和经济教育"（personal, social, health, and economic education，简称 PSHE），于 20 世纪 80 年代兴起于英国，这是一种课程，旨在帮助学生形成良好的生活方式，与人建立良好的人际关系，培养学生的责任心、自信心、社会适应性，促进作为个体及社会一员的学生身心健康发展，为成为一个积极的好公民做好充分准备。

生词点睛

secondary *adj.* 第二的；中等的	under... heading 在某标题下；属于……范畴
preferable *adj.* 更好的，更可取的	cover *v.* 包括；涉及

重点表达

❖ set out 规划；展现；开始；出发

It was raining when we **set out**. 我们出发时正下着雨。

❖ a big step 迈出了一大步

Pheebs, that's okay. You took **a big step** today. 菲比，没关系啦。你已经跨出一大步了。

Para. 3 Since official guidance on sex education was last updated in 2000 there is, as the education secretary, Damian Hinds, has acknowledged, much catching up to do. In particular, the role of technology requires urgent attention. Schools already make efforts to promote online safety, by alerting parents to the risks posed by unsuitable content, and encouraging them to reflect on how much time children spend using screens. It makes sense to instruct children in such issues directly, and supply them with the tools to think about their behaviour.

译文 正如教育部长达米安·海因兹所承认的那样，自从2000年对性教育的官方指南进行最后一次更新以来，还有很多工作要做。尤其需要迫切注意科技的影响。学校提醒家长注意网络上不当的内容可能带来的风险，并鼓励他们反思孩子花在电子设备上的时间，借此来努力促进网络安全。直接向孩子们讲授这类问题，并为他们提供思考自身行为的工具是有意义的。

生词点睛

update *v.* 更新	alert *v.* 使警觉，使警惕；使注意
unsuitable *adj.* 不合适的；不适宜的	acknowledge *v.* 承认

重点表达

❖ make efforts to 努力做……

We're **making efforts to** alleviate poverty and build a moderately prosperous society in all respects. 我们现在正在努力脱贫，共同奔小康。

❖ pose risks to 给……带来风险

Standing by as the dollar falls does **pose risks to** the U.S. 对美元下跌袖手旁观确实会给美国带来风险。

❖ reflect on 仔细考虑，思考；反省

We should often **reflect on** our past mistakes. 我们应当经常反省自己过去的错误。

❖ supply sb. with sth. 给某人提供某物

Foreign governments **supplied** the rebels **with** arms. 一些外国政府向反叛者提供武器。

拓 supply sth. to sb. 向某人提供某物

Foreign governments **supplied** arms **to** the rebels. 一些外国政府向反叛者提供武器。

Para. 4 The crisis in young people's mental health is well documented. It would be glib to suggest that revisions to the curriculum offer any kind of solution to a problem that has been out of control, and been greatly exacerbated by cuts to both national and local mental health services. But that is not to say that schools are helpless. It is a good idea to teach young people how to talk about their emotions, how to recognise symptoms of anxiety or depression, and how to access professional help.

译文 年轻人的心理健康危机已经得到了充分的证明。如果有人认为，对课程进行修订能够解决已经失控的、因为国家和地方心理健康服务削减而严重恶化的问题，那将是肤浅的。但这并不是说学校（的教育）是无用的。教授年轻人如何表达自身情绪、如何识别焦虑或抑郁的症状，以及如何获得专业的帮助是个好主意。

生词点睛

documented adj. 备有证明文件的	**glib** adj. 未经思考的；肤浅的
curriculum n.（学校等的）全部课程	**exacerbate** v. 使加剧；使恶化
symptom n. 症状	**access** v. 使用；获取

重点表达

❖ out of control 失控

Things were a little **out of control**. 当时事情有点失控。

Para. 5 As with the sensible package announced by Mr. Hinds last month to address teacher shortages, the devil of these proposals is in the details of their funding. None of what has been promised will be delivered to the required standard unless the government increases its paltry offer of £6m. Beyond the nuts and bolts of the facts of life, these are issues that require well-informed and sensitive handling: sexual orientation, gender identity, self-harm and abuse are deeply personal and difficult subjects to tackle in a classroom.

译文 就像上个月海因兹先生宣布解决教师短缺问题的合理方案一样，这些建议的难点在于资金的细节方面。除非政府提高其微不足道的 600 万英镑的报价，否则任何已作出的承诺都不会按标准要求执行。除了生活各方面的基本要点，还需要熟知一些问题并予以谨慎对待，比如：性取向、性别认同、自残和虐待都是非常私人的问题，在课堂上很难解决。

生词点睛

package n. 一套建议	**devil** n. 极难对付的事物
paltry adj. 可忽略不计的；微小的	**beyond** prep. 超出；除……之外
well-informed adj.（对某一问题）非常熟悉的	**self-harm** n. 自我伤害，自残

重点表达

❖ the nuts and bolts 具体细节，基本要点

The top leaders are always well-known, but not those who work with **the nuts and bolts**. 这些高级领袖都是被人们熟知的，但那些做基本工作的就默默无闻了。

词意选选看

1. applaud ____
2. preferable ____
3. documented ____
4. glib ____

a. 使加剧；使恶化
b. 一套建议
c. 可忽略不计的；微小的
d. 未经思考的；肤浅的

5. exacerbate ____
6. access ____
7. package ____
8. paltry ____
9. beyond ____
10. tackle ____

e. 备有证明文件的
f. 处理
g. 更好的，更可取的
h. 赞同；称赞
i. 超出；除……之外
j. 使用；获取

拓展阅读

英国家长反对将性和健康教育纳入课堂

The British government's announcement of new guidelines for sex and health education across England comes amid a backlash from parent groups who do not want it to be a mandatory part of the curriculum. Relationships, cybersafety, and mental health are all set to be included as part of the new syllabus in schools across the nation. Parliament was set to debate a petition on demanding parents retain the right to opt their child out of the classes. More than 100,000 people have stressed parents' "fundamental right" to decide when their children are taught the topics.

延伸思考： 将性和健康教育纳入课堂是否应征得学生家长的同意？

第8天

Big pharma is under fire. This week the bosses of seven large drug firms were hauled before the United States Congress to answer pointed questions about the cost of their medicines. The hearings come amid rising bipartisan anger about high drug prices. New laws are threatened. Concerns about the affordability of medicines are not peculiar to America; they are global. In Britain the price of a new drug for cystic fibrosis has provoked fury, as has the government's refusal to pay it. Italy is calling for the World Health Organisation to bring greater transparency to the cost of making drugs and the prices charged for them.

Too rarely raised in this discussion is one promising area where pillmakers and governments alike could do more to fight disease while also saving money. Drugs can be "repurposed". That is, existing drugs can sometimes be used to treat diseases other than the ones for which they were first designed. This can be a cheaper way to develop new treatments. It could also help answer another criticism often thrown at drug firms: that they do not invest enough in areas where medical need is great but financial returns are unattractive, such as rare cancers, new antibiotics and medicines for children or poor countries.

Drugmakers have a point when they say that the cost of developing new drugs for non-lucrative ailments is prohibitive. (They say it costs more than $2 bn to bring a new molecule from laboratory to pharmacy shelf.) Drug repurposing is cheaper because the drugs in question have already been tested for safety, which is itself hugely expensive. Repurposed drugs must be tested principally for effectiveness against the new disease.

Given the untapped potential in the 9,000 generic drugs (ie, those which no longer have patent protection) found in America alone, this could be just the beginning. One charity says it has found evidence of anti-cancer activity in almost 260 drugs that treat other conditions. An academic reckons that one in five existing cancer drugs might be effective against other cancers.

For all its promise, however, repurposing is underfunded. Once a drug has lost its patent protection, it is difficult for a drug firm to recoup the investment needed to test and relabel it for a new purpose. The leads already identified need to be tested with randomised trials, and then approved by regulators for their new uses. A doctor can prescribe a pill for "off label" uses without such trials. But patients may not trust a drug that is not approved for their condition; doctors may worry about being sued; and health services and insurers may be reluctant to pay for it.

文章大意

第一段：指出大型制药公司因高药价受到了美国政府和民众的猛烈批评。
第二段：指出药物使用的新领域。
第三段：说明重新利用药物成本较低。
第四段：实践证明药物可以被重新利用。
第五段：指出实现药物再利用会面临的问题。

逐段精讲

Para. 1 Big pharma is under fire. This week the bosses of seven large drug firms were hauled before the United States Congress to answer pointed questions about the cost of their medicines. The hearings come amid rising bipartisan anger about high drug prices. New laws are threatened. Concerns about the affordability of medicines are not peculiar to America; they are global. In Britain the price of a new drug for cystic fibrosis has provoked fury, as has the government's refusal to pay it. Italy is calling for the World Health Organisation to bring greater transparency to the cost of making drugs and the prices charged for them.

译文 大型制药公司受到了猛烈批评。本周，七家大型制药公司的老板被拉到美国国会面前，回答有关其药品成本的尖锐问题。听证会召开之际，两党对高药价的愤怒日益高涨。新法律受到威胁。对药品可负担性的担忧并非美国独有，而是全球性的普遍状况。在英国，一种治疗囊性纤维化的新药价格引起了民众的愤怒，政府也拒绝支付费用。意大利呼吁世界卫生组织提高药品制造成本和药价的透明度。

生词点睛

haul *v.* 强迫（某人）去某处	**pointed questions** 尖锐的问题
bipartisan *adj.* 两党的；涉及两党的	**affordability** *n.* 支付能力；负担能力
fury *n.* 暴怒，狂怒	

重点表达

❖ be under fire 受到严厉/猛烈批评（用于新闻报道）

The government's new medical policy **is under fire**. 政府的新医疗政策饱受批评。

❖ be peculiar to sb./sth. 为某人/某事物所特有

By sampling as many different situations as possible, researchers can reduce the chance that their observation results will **be peculiar to** a certain set of circumstances and conditions. 通过对尽可能多的不同情况进行采样，研究人员可以减少他们的观察结果受特定环境和条件影响的可能性。

Para. 2 Too rarely raised in this discussion is one promising area where pillmakers and governments alike could do more to fight disease while also saving money. Drugs can be "repurposed". That is, existing drugs can sometimes be used to treat diseases other than the ones for which they were first designed. This can be a cheaper way to develop new treatments. It could also help answer another criticism often thrown at drug firms: that they do not invest enough in areas where medical need is great but financial returns are unattractive, such as rare cancers, new antibiotics and medicines for children or poor countries.

译文 在这场讨论中很少提到一个有前景的领域，在这个领域中，制药商和政府可以做更多的事来对抗疾病，同时还能节省资金。药物可以被"调整用途"。也就是说，现有的药物有时可以用来治疗那些不是最初研制好要针对治疗的疾病。这可能是开发新疗法的一种更廉价的方式。这也有助于回应另一个经常向制药公司提出的批评意见：他们没有在医疗需求巨大但经济回报不具吸引力的领域投入足够的资金，例如罕见癌症、新抗生素以及儿童或贫穷国家所需的药物。

生词点睛

promising *adj.* 有希望的，有前途的	**treatment** *n.* 治疗，疗法
criticism *n.* 批评，批判；指责	**financial returns** 经济回报
unattractive *adj.* 不吸引人的；令人反感的	**antibiotic** *n.* 抗生素

重点表达

❖ be used to do sth. 被用来做……

There are a variety of methods that can **be used to** do this. 要达到这些目的，有各种各样的办法。

Para. 3 Drugmakers have a point when they say that the cost of developing new drugs for non-lucrative ailments is prohibitive. (They say it costs more than $2 bn to bring a new molecule from laboratory to pharmacy shelf.) Drug repurposing is cheaper because the drugs in question have already been tested for safety, which is itself hugely expensive. Repurposed drugs must be tested principally for effectiveness against the new disease.

译文 制药商表示，为治疗非营利性疾病开发新药的成本高得令人望而却步，这是有道理的。（他们说，将一种新分子从实验室带到药房货架的成本超过20亿美元。）调整用途的药物成本较低，因为这些正被讨论的药物已经通过安全测试，而药物安全测试方面的费用本身就非常高昂。调整用途的药物必须主要测试其对新疾病的疗效。

生词点睛

lucrative *adj.* 赚大钱的；获利多的	**ailment** *n.* 小病；不安
prohibitive *adj.* （费用）高得负担不起的	**molecule** *n.* [化学] 分子；微小颗粒，微粒
principally *adv.* 主要地	**effectiveness** *n.* 有效；有力

重点表达

❖ in question 正被讨论的，谈论中的

That is not the point **in question**. 那不是讨论的重点。

Para. 4 Given the untapped potential in the 9,000 generic drugs (ie, those which no longer have patent protection) found in America alone, this could be just the beginning. One charity says it has found evidence of anti-cancer activity in almost 260 drugs that treat other conditions. An academic reckons that one in five existing cancer drugs might be effective against other cancers.

译文 鉴于仅在美国就发现了9 000种仿制药（即那些不再拥有专利保护的药），这说明仿制药的生产可能只是个开始。一家慈善机构说，他们已经在近260种治疗其他疾病的药物中发现了抗癌活性的证据。一位学者认为现有的五分之一的抗癌药物可能对其他癌症有效。

生词点睛

given *prep.* 考虑到，鉴于	**untapped** *adj.* 未利用的，未开发的
generic drugs 仿制药	**anti-cancer activity** 抗癌活性
reckon *v.* 认为	

重点表达

❖ one out of five / one in five 五分之一

Fewer than **one out of five** clones survives past the first few days of life. 不到五分之一的克隆动物能活过生命的最初几天。

In some communities, nearly **one in five** folks were out of work. 在一些社区，有将近五分之一的人们失业。

Para. 5 For all its promise, however, repurposing is underfunded. Once a drug has lost its patent protection, it is difficult for a drug firm to recoup the investment needed to test and relabel it for a new purpose. The leads already identified need to be tested with randomised trials, and then approved by

译文 然而，要实现药物再利用的全部目标，其资金是不足的。一旦药物失去了专利保护，制药公司就很难收回测试与标明药物的新用途所需的投资。已经确定药物需要通过随机试验进行测试，然后由监管机构批准其

regulators for their new uses. A doctor can prescribe a pill for "off label" uses without such trials. But patients may not trust a drug that is not approved for their condition; doctors may worry about being sued; and health services and insurers may be reluctant to pay for it.

新用途。医生可以开一种"药品核准标示外使用"的药物，此药也无须进行试验。但是，病人可能不会信任一种药效未经批准的药物；医生可能担心被起诉；医疗服务和保险公司可能也不愿意为此买单。

生词点睛

underfunded *adj.*（项目、机构等）资金不足的	**patent protection** 专利保护
recoup *v.* 弥补（亏损），收回（成本）	**approve** *v.* 批准；认可
prescribe *v.* 开（药），给……开处方	**sue** *v.* 控告，控诉

重点表达

❖ it is difficult for sb. to do sth. 对某人来说做……是困难的

It is difficult for the old man **to** adjust to city life. 这个老人很难适应城市生活。

拓 it is + *adj.* + (for sb.) to do sth.

It is unwise to count on a person who always breaks his word. 指望一个经常食言的人是不明智的。

❖ be reluctant to do sth. 不愿做某事

She **was reluctant to** admit she was wrong. 她不愿承认自己有错。

词意选选看

1. prescribe _____   a. 经济回报

2. recoup _____   b. 仿制药

3. promising _____   c. 控告，控诉

4. treatment _____   d. 开（药），给……开处方

5. financial returns _____ e. （费用）高得负担不起的

6. lucrative _____   f. （项目、机构等）资金不足的

7. prohibitive _____   g. 有希望的，有前途的

8. generic drugs ____
9. underfunded ____
10. sue ____

h. 治疗，疗法
i. 赚大钱的；获利多的
j. 弥补（亏损），收回（成本）

> **·拓展阅读·**

药物再利用

Drug repurposing is an innovative approach as it provides new indications for already approved and established drugs. Due to high failure rates and cost involved in traditional drug development procedures, many pharmaceutical companies are primarily focusing on drug repurposing strategy. In Alzheimer disease (AD), existing therapeutic agents only provide symptomatic benefits and does not play a role in disease modification, therefore, an alternative strategy of repurposing can be used to inhibit neurodegeneracy process and other pathological complications.

延伸思考：将药物用于新用途的前景如何？